2 434762 21

D0279460

HOW TO BE A PROFESSIONAL GAMER

HOW TO BE A PROFESSIONAL GAMER

BY

FNATIC

with **Mike Diver**

CENTURY

1 3 5 7 9 10 8 6 4 2

Century
20 Vauxhall Bridge Road
London SW1V 2SA

Century is part of the Penguin Random House group of companies
whose addresses can be found at global.penguinrandomhouse.com

Penguin
Random House
UK

Copyright © Fnatic Limited 2016

Fnatic Limited have asserted their right to be identified as the
authors of this Work in accordance with the Copyright,
Designs and Patents Act 1988

First published in Great Britain by Century in 2016

www.penguin.co.uk

A CIP catalogue record for this book is available from the British Library.

ISBN 9781780896588

Typeset in India by Thomson Digital Pvt Ltd, Noida, Delhi
Printed and bound in Great Britain by Clays Ltd, St Ives plc

Penguin Random House is committed to a sustainable future for our
business, our readers and our planet. This book is made from Forest
Stewardship Council® certified paper.

RENFREWSHIRE COUNCIL	
243476221	
Bertrams	08/11/2017
793.920	£14.99
ERS	

Contents

1

The Essential Ingredients of Being a Professional Gamer

It might seem like a niche attraction compared to the big sports filling TV schedules and bringing big numbers to matches on a weekly basis, but don't be fooled: eSports is here, already in a big way, and it's only going to get more popular. Speak to people in the industry and they'll tell you, without hint of sarcasm, that in years to come the player base and global audience for competitive video gaming will eclipse that of many traditional sports.

Sport has evolved over time, and eSports – and gaming, more generally – is doing the same. Today it's perfectly natural for a kid to get home from school and spend hours in front of their PC, engaging in fantastical combat, or high-tension simulation play, against opponents potentially on the other side of the world. As the individual games grow in recognition, in subscribers, so their players begin to look for more information: how best to play the game; how to get ahead of their peers. And at the very top level of this tree of talent are the pro-gamers, those who earn their living travelling the world, playing video games against the best, inspiring millions.

In Europe, gaming can be seen as a very isolated, singular pursuit – it's hard to shake the awful stereotype of the kid alone in their room, the screen glowing, social life secondary to the interactive wonders before them. This is a hideously outdated perception of video gaming, however, and one only needs to look to South Korea to see how their culture of PC bangs – cafes full of connected computers, allowing for large-scale cooperative play between friends and total strangers alike – takes the at-home-alone nature of online gaming into the public space. And it's South Korean teams that have established no little dominance in many eSports disciplines, including *League of Legends*. Since Fnatic claimed the inaugural *League* World Championship in 2011, every winning team at the Worlds has come from Asia, with three of the four winners from South Korea itself. Does this success link back to the wider acceptance of gaming as a valuable way to spend one's free time? It's hard to argue against the logic of PC bang culture feeding into the world's healthiest competitive gaming scene.

Society will always grow alongside technology, and it's the younger elements of it, those who have grown up with video games all around them, who are best positioned to keep up with it. This provides eSports with the opportunity to grow almost exponentially. It also means that competition for places in professional teams will become even fiercer than it is today, pushing the overall quality of play upwards. Yet there is no obvious career ladder in eSports: this is an underdeveloped industry in comparison to traditional sports like football or basketball, where careers can begin at a very young age, perhaps only five or six years old.

In eSports, no organisation is going to take on a player before they reach their teenage years. Then they typically go straight from home into a professional organisation, missing out on the years of steady coaching that a set-up at a football club would provide, helping the player to mature as well as evolve their skills. And that's a huge jump, to go from being a talented casual player into the spotlight of top-level competitive gaming.

But knowing what qualities are absolutely essential for a pro-gamer to possess will help anyone looking to do just that, and step up to playing on stages, before an online audience of millions. Being a fast learner is vital in competitive *League of Legends*, maybe more so than any other eSport, because of how its makers, Riot Games, continually patch it. This means that the game is always being updated, its avatars – called champions – having their abilities tweaked, sometimes for the better and sometimes not. These changes alter the meta, which is how the professionals are playing the game around each patch, and even the slightest alterations can have massive consequences for a team's success.

The patches mean that a top-tier *League* player must be familiar with more than one champion. Stick with just the one and you might taste success, but a patch later and they might be nerfed – underpowered – into relative irrelevance. This keeps any team's strategy always changing, and every player needs not only to be specialised within their role, in their position, but to have a great understanding of the whole game. Each position carries with it select duties and responsibilities, and foremost among those is how they communicate with the other players around them. Having the discipline to look outside of your lane without compromising its strengths is a massively important part of being a *League* professional.

Giving and receiving criticism is something that every pro, whatever their game, has to be open to. If you're able to take advice, sometimes the hard way, it will only stand to improve your overall game; if you're able to provide it, then your teammates, assuming they're level-headed enough not to react negatively, will learn from it. *League* is not a game that can be won alone. It might have been that way during its first two seasons, but in 2016, it's the team that wins the game, not the individuals.

Speak to any *League* professional, from players to coaches, and they'll tell you that a harmonious atmosphere is so essential to a great team. Working with a player who doesn't share the ambitions of the rest of the players, or simply has the wrong mindset to fit into the meta in question, will always cause problems. They will struggle to fit into a gaming house, if that's an option, and cause friction with everyone in the organisation, from the bottom to the very top level of management. Professional *League* players are in each other's company for tens of hours every week, leaving no room for holding grudges.

Which isn't to say there's no room for flair, for individuality. Every week in the *League of Legends* Championship Series (LCS), in America and Europe, you will witness a player going off the strategy laid down by their coach and seizing a game-winning initiative. No coach can train this – it's something that either comes naturally or it doesn't, and it has a lot to do with the personality of the player. What should never happen, though, is an individual persistently taking risks and damaging their team's chances as a result – every window of opportunity requires swift analysis, lasting no more than a few seconds, and great communication between teammates can quickly qualify whether or not it's a move to make.

Whether you're playing in the Challenger Series (CS), solo queue – playing alone and teaming up with strangers for online games – or in the LCS, you can never be arrogant about your abilities. However highly you think of yourself, as even the pro-players featured in this book can testify to, there's almost always someone ahead of you. This is a team game, one in which so-called gods are few and far between. With increasing sponsorship and ever-rising levels of professionalism, eSports is becoming an industry in which long-term careers can be pursued. Major sporting organisations like football clubs Schalke 04 and Valencia are establishing their own *League of Legends* teams, and this will continue, increasing demands on players.

The key ingredient for anyone in the pro game, or hoping to get there, is never to spend too long in your comfort zone. Play in new ways, lose and learn, and you will benefit yourself and the team. Keep on learning, and defeats naturally become victories. Fnatic has seen that first hand – how patience and persistence can produce golden moments, never to be forgotten, and glory enough to fill a dozen more teams. That's the organisation's goal: to win everything. With eSports always expanding, this is going to be tougher with every passing year, but if any team is positioned to move with the times, with technology, each patch and each new breakout player, it's this one.

How To Be a Professional Gamer goes behind the scenes of Fnatic's *League of Legends* operation, and delves into the team's history, to collect indelible memories, professional advice, personal highs and lows and several anecdotes on all things *League* and eSports. Along the way, readers will learn what it takes to make it at the top level of competitive video gaming. This isn't something that anyone with a mouse and an opened-daily copy of League on their PC can achieve, as will soon enough become clear.

How to Use This Book

How To Be a Professional Gamer is a book of two distinct but complementary halves.

The first half of the book, roughly speaking, introduces absolute beginners to the world of eSports, and *League of Legends*, and to the entwined histories of each global phenomenon. These chapters will also be of interest to those who already enjoy playing the game but are not familiar with its roots, which go deep indeed – beyond the introduction of competitive play, the beta testing of *League* that began in 2009, and the establishment of its makers, Riot Games, in 2006.

This section of *How To Be a Professional Gamer* takes us all the way back to when Riot's founding pair of Brandon Beck and Marc Merrill were freshly graduated and seeking an opportunity to carve out a niche for themselves in the nascent competitive gaming sector. Not that playing video games in media-covered tournaments attracting top-level participants from around the world was a new thing in the first decade of the twenty-first century – the first publicised gaming contest was actually held in 1972, technically making this wonderfully 'new' world of eSports over forty years old.

From there, the book explores the monumental scale of *League*'s premier, seasons-climaxing competition – the

League of Legends World Championship. This knockout-format, city-hopping contest, pulling in teams from across all major *League* territories, was first won by Fnatic at its debut staging in 2011. Since then it's been the one achievement that all *League*-focused organisations set their sights on.

The book's second half, beginning at Chapter 7, digs into the hopes, dreams, pressures and stresses that both make and break today's professional gamer. We hear directly from Fnatic's *League of Legends* stars – all of the players on the EU LCS team – about how they raised their game to the level it's at today, where they're not just mixing with the best but setting new standards themselves.

And it's in this second half of the book where *League* regulars will find guidance for improving their results. Every member of Fnatic's first-team roster has advice for gamers looking to take their own performance up several notches – simple tips for setting themselves apart from the pack of great summoners, and into the elite. The book also explores what the future of Riot's game might be – and how Fnatic is future-proofing itself in order to stand strong against the fluctuations of the always-evolving eSports scene.

Whether you're someone who plays *League* every day – all day long, given the opportunity – or you're only just taking your first steps into its cavalcade of champions, encyclopaedia of abilities and perplexing terminology, there is something for you in *How To Be a Professional Gamer.* This book is designed to entertain and educate, and to open eyes both experienced and anew to the fascinating arena of eSports. The players might typically be young, and the infrastructure developing, but pro-gaming is exploding in popularity all around us, and accelerating. There's never been a better time to get into it.

2

What is *League of Legends,* Anyway?

League of Legends didn't just blink into life one fine day back in 2009. Its production, at the Los Angeles-headquartered Riot Games, was meticulously meditated. Some might even say that its development was spurred not by an innate desire to create for the sake of doing so on the part of its makers, fuelled by a burning passion to further this most interactive of entertainment mediums, but by competitive gaming trends of the time, a very business-minded and margins-led methodology.

League of Legends wasn't pretending to break entirely new ground in the emerging multiplayer online battle arena (MOBA) scene. Instead, it aimed to match the player base of the standout title of the time, and ultimately to surpass it in popularity by refining all of the elements that made this style of game so appealing, and by introducing compelling new ones all of its own. That market leader, or more accurately that mod – a user-made game created using custom tools – was *Defense of the Ancients*, or *DotA*. And understanding both its success and that of *League of Legends* necessitates a brief history lesson.

Warcraft III: Reign of Chaos, released in the summer of 2002, was Californian studio Blizzard Entertainment's third real-time strategy title in its *Warcraft* series. Today that franchise covers not only video games in the same style, but also the massively multiplayer online role-playing game (MMORPG) *World of Warcraft* (*WoW*) – the most successful MMORPG of all time, according to *Guinness World Records*, with over 100 million subscribers – and *Hearthstone*, a free-to-play collectible card game inspired by *Warcraft* lore, which as of spring 2016 was being played by 50 million people worldwide. Back in 2002, *Reign of Chaos* was *the* title amongst web-connected strategists with a taste for everything fantasy-flavoured, selling over a million copies in a month.

Its cast of orcs and humans, elves and the undead may have been indebted to the fiction of authors like *The Lord of the Rings* writer J. R. R. Tolkien and ancient European folklore alike, but Blizzard's combining of familiar constituents with established real-time strategy (RTS) mechanics resulted in a game that was enveloping like so few other comparable experiences of the time. The sales figures don't lie; likewise the review scores: *Reign of Chaos* was a runaway hit commercially, and it secured highly positive press coverage from the likes of *Game Informer* and *PC Gamer*, the latter calling it 'a brilliant game in every facet of its design and execution, with not a single dull moment'.

The way *Warcraft III* played only gently nudged RTS games forward in terms of functionality – you controlled units to secure new territory on a map, obliterating the enemy's own ranks to take control of their held areas, gathering construction resources and developing player-controlled 'hero' avatars as you went – but soon enough it would inspire a sea change in multiplayer gaming. Not that Blizzard themselves had much to do with it.

A Game of Clones

DotA was born from the *Warcraft III* world editor, with a modder known as Eul taking the layout of a custom map in another of Blizzard's RTS games, *StarCraft*'s triple-lane Aeon of Strife, and applying its structure to the newer game's menu of creation tools. *StarCraft*'s Aeon pitched one powerful hero against waves of enemies coming down the three lanes, but for Eul's 2003 take on it, which he titled *Defense of the Ancients*, up to five players could take on the same number on the other team, alongside two computer-controlled (or artificial intelligence (AI)) units per game. That's five on five, on a map with three clear avenues of engagement – for any existing *League of Legends* players, this is starting to sound familiar. Eul's map proved incredibly popular but was unexpectedly left behind by its maker, who elected to step away from the *DotA* scene. This allowed many others in *Warcraft*'s modding community to put their own mark on proceedings, increasingly so after *Reign of Chaos* was followed by a new expansion pack, *The Frozen Throne*, boasting brand-new world editor features.

One such modder was Guinsoo, aka Wisconsin-born game designer Steve Feak. He took over an already in-rotation *DotA* variant map, February 2004's *Allstars* by Meian and Ragn0r, which placed *Warcraft III*'s most popular heroes into combat against one another, and worked some unprecedented magic. Just a month after *Allstars*' unveiling, Feak put out a new version of the map, quickly followed by another that featured the non-player-controlled Roshan, a powerful neutral 'creep' designed to pose more of a threat than the weaker, AI-controlled characters that *DotA* teams would farm for gold – the same sort of cannon fodder as *League of Legends*' minions. Roshan would become a *DotA* mainstay, now the most powerful of all creeps in *Dota 2*, and so too would how the game played once Feak had finished his work, although another modder, Icefrog, inarguably perfected what his predecessor had left for him, tweaking the map to facilitate a wider competitive community.

DotA Allstars' basic premise was simple enough: each team, one named the Sentinel and the other the Scourge, would try to obliterate the other's base, located at the south-west or north-east of the map depending on which side you were on. These bases were protected by fortifications, towers and a range of AI-controlled units; and at their centres were 'Ancients', the destruction of which served as the end-game trigger. Bring the enemy's 'Ancient' down and you won. This gameplay would serve as a broad base for *League of Legends*, in which the 'Ancient' became the Nexus, a brilliant beacon begging to be smashed into smithereens. Obliterate your opponent's Nexus and to your team go the spoils. *League* added extra win conditions, not necessitating the fall of a Nexus, but at its heart the parallels with *DotA* are crystal clear.

Competitive *DotA Allstars* tournaments began in earnest in 2005, at that year's BlizzCon, a public convention held annually by Blizzard in support of its major franchises. Grass-roots contests had started a year earlier, with the first *Allstars* league formed in April 2004 under the banner of Clan TDA. The game's global profile was accelerated by its addition to the World Cyber Games in 2005, and the Electronic Sports World Cup in 2008, and by the summer of 2008 it was truly a phenomenon. Games industry website Gamasutra covered *DotA* that June, writer Michael Walbridge calling it 'an underground revolution' and 'a delight to all who play it'. He noted that only Valve's team-based first-person shooter *Counter-Strike* could hold a candle to *DotA* in terms of depth, fun and, most importantly, fan base. Swedish dance artist Basshunter named a 2006 song after it, which went top-ten in his home country. All of the momentum was leading to the inevitable: a *DotA* 'proper', built by a professional games studio.

And in 2010, Washington state's Valve Corporation, the studio behind *Half-Life* and its sequel *Counter-Strike*, *Portal*, *Team Fortress* and *Left 4 Dead* – all classics of their kind, as revered today as they were on release – made the announcement that everyone in the *DotA* scene had predicted. They'd be making *DotA 2*, with Icefrog as lead designer, building from the ground up a stand-alone title tailor-made for the developing eSports market. Work on the game began in 2009, and it eventually came out in July 2013. But by the time of its launch, another MOBA had established a stranglehold on competitive and casual scenes alike: *League of Legends*, a game explicitly inspired by *DotA Allstars*.

Starting a Riot

Riot Games was officially founded in 2006 by Brandon Beck and Marc Merrill, CEO and president of the company, respectively, as of July 2016. Merrill's postgraduate background was in corporate marketing, and he'd worked at financial services companies Merrill Lynch and US Bancorp. Beck, meanwhile, left a job in media and entertainment strategy at Bain & Company, a global consultancy firm, to begin what at the time was a risky venture. The pair met each other while attending the University of Southern California, in Los Angeles, and both graduated in 2004. Competitive gaming was in its infancy in the middle of the twenty-first century's first decade (some may argue that it still is, given the near-infinite space available for it to evolve into), and the pair's vision for *League*, and Riot, started more as a wouldn't-this-be-nice daydream than a determined, spreadsheeted plan, road-mapped to perfection.

Riot didn't begin in an office space of any size: the founders laid the foundations for what was to come in a shared apartment, where each had a sizeable gaming rig set up. Online, competitive gaming was in their blood, but for a while it remained a passion only, not a professional avenue of investigation and, ultimately, reward. Come the end of 2005, though, all that changed. An idea took hold of the pair: that gamers, people just like themselves, who were enraptured by this emerging world of web-connected competition and cooperative play, wanted something more than a game on a disk that as good as stopped once you'd seen out its core objectives. There was the demand for something more fluid, something more alive, something that couldn't be boxed up and shipped out, but instead continually flowed through the globe's broadband networks, free of physical form but just as rich in detail, lore, longevity and *fun* as the likes of *World of Warcraft*.

Beck and Merrill could see a future capable of changing the way online gamers played: no more lengthy waits between game updates, no more year-on-year iterations asking for more money for essentially the same experience over again. They looked outside of gaming circles for business guidance, and found it with the popular 'software as a service' (SaaS) model used by enterprise software – programs used in the workplace, for jobs including payroll processing, IT management and human resources. This SaaS model saw programs receive regular updates, which the user didn't have to leave their desk to pick up at the shop; and rather than every new version of said software costing an individual price, businesses would pay subscriptions simply to receive the updates as and when they became available, in real time. SaaS models saw the companies behind them establish two-way conversations with their clients, communities forming around software, and regular dialogue between makers and customers meant that the programs in question could be refined with direct input from the people actually using them.

This is what Beck and Merrill wanted to bring into the video gaming space: a service-orientated approach that would keep them in constant touch with the people playing the game itself, which in turn would evolve it in a way that satisfied all parties. They began to recruit. An office opened in September 2006, and into it came none other than Steve Feak, and alongside him Steve Mescon, aka Pendragon, the creator of a *DotA Allstars* community website. The concept of a spiritual successor to Feak's *DotA* map was a natural product of Riot's initial DNA, and the team didn't look back. *League of Legends* was announced in October 2008, and come January 2009 Riot had forty employees working hard to get the game off the ground, and both closed and open betas – a kind of water-testing period for the final game to come – out to an eager player base.

To help *League of Legends* stand out against *DotA* – and, indeed, *Warcraft III* and every other online multiplayer game of the time – the team at Riot began to create champions, its player-controlled (or summoner-controlled, if you will) avatars, that were so much *weirder* than much of what had come before. Fiddlesticks, 'the Harbinger of Doom', was a scarecrow-like mage capable of casting dread and fear on the enemy; Annie, 'the Dark Child', went into battle beside a demonic teddy-*ish* bear by the name of Tibbers; and Soraka was a healer from the stars, a celestial once-immortal whose aggression stripped her of everlasting life. They're all still in there, playable today. Every character, and the game featured forty at its 2009 beta launch (at the time of writing there are 131), had a compelling backstory woven into detailed lore telling of the Rune Wars that ravaged the land of Valoran, and the Fields of Justice upon which winner-takes-all battles were now to be waged.

But this layering of aesthetic qualities and background fiction wouldn't guarantee *League*'s long-term survival. Riot recognised that gameplay alone would be the determining factor there, and that *DotA* was proving this well enough. So, it stood to reason that a fresh twist on Feak's *Allstars* map built in a new proprietary engine, supported by a high level of customer service, fresh-to-the-scene in-game features and exemplary community communication would be a recipe for getting results. And so it would prove, once the game slipped free of its beta phases and became available as a finished product, albeit one that would go on to be patched regularly, in order to balance champions and refresh play styles.

By July 2011, *League of Legends* had 15 million registered players worldwide, ahead of *Warcraft*'s 12 million, making it one of the biggest PC games of all time. Well over a million of those players were logging on every single day, adding up to an accumulative total of 3.7 million hours spent on the Fields of Justice every twenty-four hours. The growth of the game's community outstripped all expectations. But no laurels were about to be rested on. Speaking to the tech website Engadget in the summer of 2011, Beck said, 'We are proud of the numbers we are hitting on our platform and are confident our fantastic team can continue to grow and evolve our . . . technology to handle even greater numbers.'

Gauntlet thrown, but the confidence has been vindicated: in early 2014, 67 million people had registered with the game, and more than 27 million worldwide were playing *League* on a daily basis, 7.5 million of them simultaneously during peak periods. And while Riot hasn't released any official figures for 2015 or 2016, 334 million people in total watched the four-week conclusion to the 2015 *League of Legends* World Championship, covering the quarters to the Berlin-staged final itself. The climax at the Mercedes-Benz Arena – contested between the ultimately victorious SK Telecom T1 (SKT) and KOO Tigers (now known as ROX Tigers) – was watched by 36 million unique viewers, a new record across the whole of the eSports sector.

Evidently, mainstream, casual-level enthusiasm for *League* is far from on the wane, just as the professional side of the game achieves new peaks of competitiveness and prize money – SKT walked away from the German capital in 2015 with a million US dollars added to the team's already healthy kitty.

Would You Like to Play a Game?

League of Legends, then, is a five-against-five, multiplayer online battle arena game, in which the player assumes the role of a summoner – to use the game's vernacular for the godlike controllers of the champions in battle, i.e.

you – and works alongside their teammates to destroy the enemy Nexus. Sounds simple. And the game's availability as a free download – it uses a microtransactions model to sell new champions, boosts and skins (avatar outfits), but progressing in the game does not necessitate any payment whatsoever – ensures that anyone, or at least anyone with a halfway dependable personal computer, can try it out to see if it fits their gaming tastes.

But getting into the game for the long term, as opposed to getting into a game just to run about and murder some minions, isn't quite so simple. *League* is far from an easy game to jump into, versus other competitive online multiplayer offerings like those based on real-life football/soccer, and the one-on-one fighter scene, presenting to the absolute beginner a cavalcade of confusing characters, abilities, perks, stats and stages. It has a language all of its own, spanning champions, move-sets, shoutcaster (commentator) colloquialisms and in-progress measurements of who's winning and who most certainly isn't.

There are a host of 'beginner's guides' to *League of Legends* online, but to condense what's out there on the web into a succinct couple of paragraphs on how to take your first steps in the game, in such a way that you'll make the journey again, here are the basics.

23

First, spend *nothing*, to begin with: select an already-unlocked champion and don't worry about what position they're best suited to. Ideally stick with that champion for the foreseeable, too – later in this book, this very advice will be dished out by one of Fnatic's finest, so don't ignore it. Where they're best suited to on the map – on the main Summoner's Rift map, the same you see in competition play – will become obvious the more you play, with support characters naturally gravitating towards the bottom lane and tanks to the top.

Allow yourself up to an hour per game – *League* doesn't stop when a whistle blows, and if that Nexus is holding out, and the enemy is in fine defensive form, you're going to be there a while. Even when on the front foot, on the doorstep of the enemy's base, make sure you keep your side's minions in front of you – they're a great sponge for tower fire. Keep an eye on the map – you'll want to know where your teammates are both for when you need assistance, and for when they do. And do, if you can, speak to them, using *League*'s in-game text – but be aware of the Summoner's Code, which is Riot's list of rules regarding behaviour during games. In a nutshell: be supportive and kind, and refrain from using explicit, offensive language. The more you play, the higher your individual (player profile) level will become, and more options become available.

Initially, you'll only be able to play against AI-controlled opposition, and while that might sound dull, it's important to learn the ropes. *Learn the ropes.*

This book will help with that, with Fnatic's *League* team offering plenty of positional advice in upcoming chapters. But no one guide can truly teach you how to play Riot's runaway hit – you have to get in there for yourself and find what's comfortable, and then switch from that happy place in order to challenge yourself, and improve. That's how the pros have always done it, and it's worked pretty spectacularly for them.

3

The Lore of a Legend:
League's Own History

Competitive video games aren't especially known for their stories. The reasons *why* a particular sack of sinew and sweat is smacking a rival in the chops in your average one-on-one fighter – be that something from the *Street Fighter* or *Mortal Kombat* series, or any of the numerous fighting games currently benefitting from healthy competitive communities – tend to get in the way of the action, come high-tension knockout play. At that point, at tournaments such as the annual Evolution Championship Series in Las Vegas and the rolling Capcom Pro Tour, the stories that matter are those that exist between the players themselves, not their chosen avatars: the previous encounters, the tightly contested bout of this time last year, the racing up the ranking table versus the plummeting the other way.

But of course, anyone who's played a *Street Fighter* or a *Mortal Kombat* game in the calm and quiet of their own home – rather than before a screaming and cheering crowd of several thousand, each one frantically awaiting the match-winning knockout blow – knows there is a story to these things. Often there are several, with each character having their own narrative within a wider, overarching tale that binds everything together. And as game series age, so this body of lore expands to encompass all manner of new personnel, and just occasionally a total rebooting of everything that's already come to pass. This is just as true of *League of Legends* as it is of the seemingly never-ending battles of Ryu and Ken et al. *League* might not feature a cast of obviously connected characters, its 131 (at the time of writing) champions, to look at them in terms of both aesthetics and how they play in any selected arena; but each and every one of them has their place on the supercontinent of Valoran.

Fight for Your Right

Speaking to the website warcry.com in January 2009, Marc Merrill laid out the very basic background behind why all of these champions are at each other's throats. His simple, succinct summary, dating from before the game escaped its beta phase, reads as follows:

For centuries, the Rune Wars ravaged the nations and resources of Valoran, decimating populations and wrenching the earth with maelstroms of arcane magic. In the wake of such destruction and desolation, the nations rallied together and assembled the Institute of War, a multinational governing body that would settle all disputes and put an end to centuries-old fighting.

Within the Institute of War lies the League of Legends, where powerful magic users and delegates from each realm assemble to vie for the chance to rule the land. There are no long-winded speeches or ornately drafted documents. Conflicts are resolved on the Fields of Justice, where head-to-head combat between teams of highly trained champions decides the fate of the universe. The stakes are high with the balance of power shifting with every victory or defeat. With the lives of millions of citizens on the line, there is only one rule among those in the league: winner rules all.

Sounds simple enough, but while the action is at its core fairly elementary, with two teams of five kicking each other until one or the other team's base falls, the individual stories of each champion certainly aren't. And while there isn't space in this book to dive into the details of every single one, looking at a handful of the original forty, released at the game's debut, and how they fit into these Rune Wars, illustrates just how deep the story side of *League* actually goes, if you're prepared to poke around in its multifaceted plotline for a while.

But first of all, those Rune Wars: what were they all about, anyway? In a proverbial nutshell, Valoran – which is the major land mass of a planet that's far from our own, by the name of Runeterra – has played unfortunate host to two major outbreaks of dangerous magic users going head to head with each other in countless numbers. This left the landscape fractured, scarred and unstable, both physically and politically. In response, the summoners of Valoran, effectively the leading politicians in the game's fiction (and also the role the players adopt, commanding their champions from a top-down perspective), banded together to form the League of Legends – a controllable method of resolving conflict between the land's various races.

These 'winner rules all' contests, designed to settle all major political disagreements, would be played out on specially created Fields of Justice – and the map seen in competitive *League* the world over is one of these, Summoner's Rift. The basic rules of combat we covered in the previous chapter.

Remixing the Original Champions

At *League*'s launch, forty playable champions were available. Today, fitting them into suitable positions on the Rift doesn't follow the same pattern as it did when they first emerged. Patches have reformatted these characters' abilities, buffing them or nerfing them – which is to say, amplifying or weakening their powers, accordingly.

For example, let's look at Evelynn, aka 'the Widowmaker', an assassin-type champion who is said, as per the deep lore attached to all characters, to hail from the haunted lands of Runeterra's Shadow Isles, located to the south-east of Valoran. At launch, her 'Hate Spike' ability was a spammable attack that took damage off a couple of nearby enemies; today, however, this has transformed into a single-direction line of spikes that rise out of the ground, only affecting enemies that are stepping across her line of sight. Her 'Ravage' ability has also been altered, once a single blow and now a double-slash attack that can be chained for rising damage.

Veigar, part of the nomadic, metre-tall yordle race of south-eastern Valoran, twisted into evil by encounters with dark wizards, once possessed the 'Entropy' power, which would steal ability points from rivals and award them to himself. Today, that skill is gone completely, re-inforcing the need both to keep up to date with champions come every patch Riot lays down on the game, and to vary your champion selection as much as possible.

Evelynn and Veigar are both fairly traditional-look-ing fantasy characters, following precedents laid down long before Riot was founded: both are humanoid, with the former blue-skinned, barely clothed and male-gaze-conformingly lithe, and the latter *League*'s own nefarious version of the black mages from Square's *Final Fantasy* series, a class crystallised by the look of *Final Fantasy IX*'s glowing-eyed Vivi Ornitier. But even among the first batch of *League* champions, some avatar designs were unlike anything seen in video games before. As men-tioned before, partially this was due to a need to stand separate from *DotA*, but a great deal of work goes into not only making each champion singularly appealing when it comes to their place in the game's world, but also how they look and act on the Fields of Justice.

31

The Making of a Champion

Speaking to USGamer.net in October 2014, just ahead of the *League* World Championship final in Seoul, Riot's senior animator Rory Alderton revealed a little about the background to making a champion come to life. He explained to writer Mike Williams that Riot has four animation teams, and they collaborate to keep every new avatar, or each update, looking fresh and, pertinently, unique against everything else on screen. As with most design processes, the creative juices first flow into concept drawings, which inform everything that follows.

> After the concept phase, [the design] goes to the modeler who will make a proxy model . . . a temp model that they can quickly make, sometimes in a day. That gets sent to the rigger, who puts the skeletal infrastructure in . . . It can then go to the animator . . . That's how the pipeline works . . .
>
> It's hard to put an exact timeline on [the time it takes to make each champion], because you can be working on [one] and someone will feel that something is just not right. We never like to release things until we're absolutely happy with them. A gut-check would be around four months. It all depends on the

complexity of the champion. Sometimes champions are in the . . . concept phase for years.

IN SEPTEMBER 2015, Riot mechanics designer August Browning spoke to PC Gamer's Shaun Prescott about how any given champion's abilities are built into their character from the very ground up, alongside the processes of the art department.

I'm working really closely with the writer and the concept artist. We give each other constant feedback about how [the champions] feel in-game, how they look compared to how they feel, and we work together to make the most cohesive character possible . . . It's very much a team effort . . .

Balancing new characters, especially when we're trying to make them new and different, is really hard. The crazier the champion is . . . the less baselines we have to go off . . .

One of the big things is that we understand we're not going to get a champion perfectly balanced when we release them, but we can be very responsive when they come out . . . Then we can buff up or nerf [them] accordingly.

When It All Goes Wrong

Browning's admission that Riot doesn't always get its champions quite right at the first opportunity is a feeling anecdotally echoed by many a player, professional and casual alike. And so too is the fact that even when updating champions, to bring a greater balance to their place in the game, not everything is always going to go according to plan. Their regular updating of champion attributes, abilities and looks can send some fans of the game reeling. In early 2016, Fiora, the rapier-wielding 'Grand Duelist' from the Kingdom of Demacia, in the west of Valoran, had her looks altered, and quite a furore followed.

On the official *League of Legends* boards, there was dissent regarding updated outfits, or skins, that players had purchased for her. 'This is definitely not the skin I bought,' posted the user 'FelRain'. 'Why is everything so oversized and flamboyant?' Beyond the aesthetic change, there were problems with the champion's skill set: 'I'm not even going to go into details on how a duelist is now a support bruiser,' commented the same user. Another, posting as 'Buffy', wrote: 'holy crap, what a downgrade.' But players don't pay for a champion's skills, selecting four from a spread of several more – they spend their money on dressing their chosen few favourites how they wish, which is why Riot has to tread carefully around cosmetic updates that could antagonise paying customers.

In response to the negative reaction to Fiora's new look, Riot's senior concept artist at the time, Michael Maurino, took to Reddit to explain the situation affecting *League* across the board:

> We are updating some of the assets to adjust for more of a softer take. Some tweaks are being made to the [Fiora] model to decrease some of the angular-ness as well as soften some facial features. That's happening across skins as well.
>
> To make a long story short, we have a lot of design philosophies surrounding characters as [they relate to] read, clarity, hierarchy, intellectual property development and world building, and creating distinctiveness in the roster. There are very deliberate decisions we make along the way of any character design.

Fiora is far from the only champion whose redesign was met by a less-than-positive player base, or at least when judged by responses to Maurino's Reddit post. One user, commenting as 'cuddlysatan', replied: 'You would do well to remember that not everyone is into [your artistic direction], and adjust accordingly, because you're tampering with someone's experiences when you change only for yourself and not for the audience.'

US Gamer staff writer Mike Williams penned an opinion piece expressing his thoughts on *League*'s fan base's ire at Fiora's redesign in January 2016.

If you dislike what a creator has done . . . you *should* make your voice heard. As long as you do so in a civil manner, rock out. More speech is a good thing . . .

We are all customers or potential customers; it only makes sense to offer our input into the development process. But it's disingenuous to say the creator must be unfettered only when it's not beneficial to you . . .

League of Legends is a commercial work and every choice is a compromise of creative and business realities . . . Riot made a design choice for creative and gameplay reasons. Now they must decide if further changes or a reversion is needed.

In this case, [it's] said that it hears the feedback from fans.

At the time of writing, Fiora's model remains the 'altered' design. Which perhaps seems like her makers are not being rightfully responsive to their audience's needs, but there are two points to remember. First, the most vocal of gamers online often represent a minority opinion, at least in the sense that the greatest number of Fiora players have simply adapted to her update just as they have any number of patches across *League*'s lifespan. Second, with over 130 champions to manage, an already updated avatar is unlikely to be top of the pecking order when, inevitably, several others are constantly in need of rebalancing to reflect the latest patch, so as to best fit the present meta – everything playing out beneath the basics of the win-or-lose scenario, from pre-play strategies to champion drafting, or the game *outside* of the game.

The long and the short of it is that Riot will never, ever be able to keep every one of its millions of players happy, with every champion playing as perfectly as its core users demand. No amount of staff in the world could pull that off, with the overall game changing so frequently. This is just another reason why the pro-players specialise in more than a single champion, varying their drafts to best suit the present meta and how the opposition is lining up, while considering bans as best they can. One thing that does affect every player's enjoyment of *League*, though, is its arenas, the Fields of Justice: get those wrong, and the very core of the competition begins to crumble.

Fields of Change

Summoner's Rift is the arena that most *League* players call home. Set in a forest in an area of Valoran where magic is abundant, between the Iceborn-ruled northern lands of Freljord and the largely unexplored Ironspike Mountains, this is a Field of Justice where the local fauna has become dangerously affected by the supernatural powers surrounding it. Four different elemental dragons spawn in the area at different times of each game, with the incredibly dangerous Elder Dragon appearing after thirty-five minutes of play; while a powerful Blue Sentinel, sharing the map along with various smaller but potentially lethal monsters, can easily crush unwary champions. It's a place of combat where attention must be closely paid not only to the opposition, attacking from the opposite corner, but its wealth of native nasties, eager to trim health off any passing player.

Summoner's Rift is the most popular map, the sole fighting ground of competitive *League*. But there is also Twisted Treeline, a horizontal arena with two lanes and a middle jungle hiding a deadly neutral monster, the huge undead spider Vilemaw. Of the map, Riot co-founder Marc Merrill commented in 2009: 'It's really well designed to force action to the middle of the map, for a three on three experience.' Due to the smaller team size, it's not a map that features in the LCS – it's far easier to achieve balanced matches when you're playing five against five. On this lack of pro-game support, Daniel Klein, a champion designer at Riot, posted a comment on the official *League of Legends* forum in 2012:

> The reason pros don't play [Twisted Treeline] is that there's no money in it. All the money's in SR [Summoner's Rift]. This is also the reason you don't see the pros play Dominion. If you want to stay at the top of the game, you've got to play massive amounts of SR every day. This is a bit of a chicken and egg problem: there are no prized events in non-SR because no pro gamers are interested, and no pro-gamers are interested in non-SR because there are no prized events. There's solutions to this problem, of course, but no easy or quick ones.

Which suggests that, in 2012, it was Riot's intention to adjust Twisted Treeline to make it as popular as Summoner's Rift, or at least occasionally featured in high-profile, top-level competition play. That hasn't happened, but Twisted Treeline remains popular among sets of casual players – and, according to Klein, some pro-players do dip in and out of it when not focused on scrimming in Summoner's Rift. What's not playable today is the Field of Justice called Crystal Scar, on which the aforementioned Dominion games were hosted. This required teams of five to capture and hold select points of a circular map for as long as possible, fending off the opposition's attempts to claim it for themselves, with each passing second dealing damage to the enemy Nexus.

Launched in September 2011, Crystal Scar, and the Dominion play mode, were designed to encourage fast-turnaround games full of exciting skirmishes. But with Summoner's Rift so dominant, ultimately Riot had to cease support for a map, and a mode, that simply weren't doing the numbers for them. Game modes lead designer at Riot, Rowan Parker, broke the news to fans through the official *League of Legends* website in February 2016:

We want to support game modes delivering consistently engaging and competitive experiences. Fewer than 0.5% of players actively play Dominion . . .
In the absence of our attention . . . game quality in [it] varies wildly based on daily engagement . . .
We might have been able to break out of that downward spiral with more dedicated resources, but we chose Summoner's Rift as the core *League of Legends*

experience with its depth of gameplay, match pacing, and path to mastery . . .

We've learned a lot from Dominion and the costs associated with maintaining a fully separate game mode . . . [but now w]e're retiring [it] to focus on our vision for *League* moving forward.

Which is Rift, Rift and more Rift – there's another five-on-five map in the game, Howling Abyss, comprising one large central lane and no jungle, but much like Twisted Treeline it never gets a professional look in. But the Rift of 2016 is not the same one seen at the game's launch, having undergone two periods of substantial change between then and now.

Summoner's Redux

A graphical and technical update took place in May 2012, ahead of a massive overhaul in 2014, at the end of that year's LCS season. The basic structure of the Rift has remained as it was in 2009: three lanes, two Nexus targets, five versus five on the field itself. Farm gold, kill creeps, level up – same as it ever was.

The updates of 2012 were papering over cracks, really; bucketing the water out until some more meaningful fixes

could come into play. Champion models were updated –
as always, with a mixed reception – alongside upgraded
environment textures right across the Rift. Jungle-lurking
neutral monsters – the dragons, the Sentinel, the fero-
cious Baron Nashor – gained improved animations, and
the game was modified to run smoother on low- to mid-
spec computers.

Then came the big shift to the map Riot's staffers have
been known to call 'ol' trusty'. The new Rift went live on
12 November 2014 for Team Builder and bot modes,
and then a week later it completely replaced the older
model. The most immediately noticeable change was the
arena's art style, which took on a more handcrafted look.
Everything became easier to read, with less in the way of
environmental clutter. The purple team became red, so
as to better differentiate champions against their blue
enemies, and each team's jungle took on a corresponding
hue; the game's camera angle was shifted slightly, allowing
for a higher perspective on the action. The update brought
new monster icons, kill indicators, new-look shopkeepers
for champions to purchase game-changing items from,
and new music.

Riot's Andrew Brownell, product lead on all things
League of Legends, explained in a 2014 blog post that the
company's five key points for making the Rift changes

were 'clarity and readability', 'visual fidelity', 'gameplay', 'thematic cohesion' and 'performance', adding: 'When a fraction of a second can mean the difference between life and death, it's critical the game delivers the most import-ant information at any given moment, in ways that are as clear and easy to understand as possible.' So while the updated Rift was – *is* – undeniably a more attrac-tive place to play than its previous guise, the changes Riot introduced were spearheaded by the desire to refine the gameplay, rather than simply make everything look prettier. The response was incredibly positive: comments beneath Brownell's post included 'It looks great!' and 'Simply amazing'. Of course, once the champions them-selves began to shift to a complementary art style, there would be some unrest, but what's that old adage about making an omelette, again?

The Ideal Starters

One of the biggest challenges facing a newcomer to *League of Legends* is who to take into battle on the Fields of Justice. Later in this book, Fnatic's professionals will provide some tips of their own regarding each role in the game, but if you want to jump in before then, here's who's recom-mended for each position by the gaming press, as based on posts from Kotaku.com in 2015, and PCGamesN.com in early 2016.

On Kotaku, writer Yannick LeJacq recommends trying all the positions – top, middle and AD carry in the bottom lane, support and jungler – but to ultimately 'focus on one'. He warns against starting out with jungler intentions, though, writing: 'It's a more specialized role than the other positions – one that requires specific skills, experience, champions, and in-game items. The first three of those only really come with time.' He says that while there are several online guides to individual champions, there are not 'step-by-step instruction manuals', given that a character might play a certain way in this role, and quite differently in another, assuming they've the base flexibility for multitasking.

PCGamesN outlines 'top champions' for each position, with their picks broken down as follows: Maokai ('one of the strongest top-laners right now') and Ekko ('a really fun champion to play') for top lane; Ahri ('easy to get to grips with') and Morgana ('a very strong skillset') for the middle; and Caitlyn ('you'll be feeling her worth long before the late game') and Lucian ('focused on persistently getting damage down on his foe') as ideal AD carry champions for taking along the bottom. Its support picks are Braum ('his skillset focuses on protecting his teammates') and Leona ('going full YOLO can be super fun'); junglers Vi (a 'made to measure jungler') and Graves ('his jungle viability has skyrocketed') receive the site's seal of approval.

In the 2016 LCS Summer Split, Fnatic's finest have dipped into some of these champions themselves. At the time of writing, top-laner Kikis has taken Ekko out for one winning game, likewise Maokai. In the jungle, Spirit experimented with Graves just the once, albeit with a losing result. Mid-laner Febiven has steered clear of the beginner-recommended champions – his favourites of Azir and Viktor are, in his words, 'best suited to people with experience'. YellOwStaR has selected Braum no fewer than nine times as his support choice, while Rekkles' AD carry champion has been Lucian four times, and Caitlyn once.

This shows that while there are some champions that are perhaps easier to immediately understand the skill set of, it doesn't really make them entry-level-only options – at the very highest level of competitive *League* play, every champion in the game can do a job when the situation suits it. So every time a forum explodes with accusations of one character or another being overpowered, nerfed into pointlessness or outright irrelevant in the current meta, it's worth remembering that this state of play can change with the very next patch.

'The game is always changing, and you always have to pick the best champion for your role,' says YellOwStaR. 'Maybe over the course of a year, as a professional, you might play as seven or eight champions. For newcomers, starting the game now, they can be overwhelmed. New players have so much to learn – and they might not like it. But when you get to know what's going on, and how all the systems work, you'll probably enjoy it.'

4

The Rise of Fnatic and Professional *League of Legends*

Competitive gaming and the world that we now know as eSports didn't begin with *League of Legends*, *DotA*, *Hearthstone* or any kind of online title. Fnatic might have been amongst the first major organisations to really make a name for itself in this industry within an industry, but the company's founding in July 2004 took place decades after video games were first used in a tournament-style fashion, where elite players took on their peers for more than mere bragging rights.

The first video gaming tournament that received any kind of widespread publicity happened all the way back in

October 1972, when the 'Intergalactic Spacewar Olympics' was held at Stanford University's Artificial Intelligence Laboratory. The competition, advertised with the promise of free beer, featured two formats, both played on the game that gave the event its name, the 1962-developed *Spacewar!*: a five-man free-for-all, and a more structured, team-based knockout contest in which participants paired up. The latter was won by Slim Tovar and Robert E. Maas, and the single-player competition by Bruce Baumgart; they all won a year's subscription to *Rolling Stone* magazine, whose Annie Leibovitz was in attendance to take photos, and the honour of being the world's first-ever eSports champions.

In the summer of 1980, Twin Galaxies was established, an organisation to keep tabs on the players who were registering the highest scores in the booming arcade game scene. In 1983, it assisted in the founding of the US National Video Game Team, which toured the States and overseas, promoting the appeal of video games as well as taking part in and hosting a raft of international tournaments.

Throughout the 1980s, the *Guinness World Records* team monitored the greatest achievements in the still-nascent field of video games, documenting the exploits of emerging superstars of the arcade, like *Donkey Kong* and *Pac-Man* top-scorer Billy Mitchell, the proud owner of gaming's most iconic mullet. In the same decade, watching video games, as well as playing them, became a pastime that television networks took an interest in, with US TV show *Starcade* broadcasting arcade challenges throughout 1982 and 1983 – long before the celebrities-loaded *GamesMaster* arrived in the UK in 1992, and practically a lifetime ahead of the Twitch and YouTube streams we use today. In 1990, Nintendo held its first world championships – the event returned in 2015, during that year's E3 – and defunct movie-rental company Blockbuster ran a world championships of its own featuring games played on various platforms.

Online Opportunities

The rising popularity of online video games in the 1990s enabled titles like *Quake* and *Counter-Strike* to break out of casuals-only play and into competitive territories. The latter, originally created as a *Half-Life* mod before being properly acquired and developed by Valve, caught the attention of a young Swede who would go on to dominate the game at tournament level between 2006 and 2012, when it was played in its *CS 1.6* version (in other words, six patches on from its original release).

'*Counter-Strike* changed my life,' says Patrik Sättermon, Fnatic's chief gaming officer today and one of the first-person shooter's truly legendary players. 'I started playing when I was fourteen or fifteen, at the same time as playing a lot of other sports, mainly football, back in Sweden. I was very into keeping myself active and fit. I played some Nintendo games, but once we had broadband in our house, I'd spend hours on my brother's PC, and I found that *Counter-Strike* satisfied my appetite for competition, and gave me all that same excitement of being part of a team. I played it as much as I could, close to 24/7 – any time, really, as all I had to do was turn on the PC. I started to climb the ladder – only for fun because the idea then of eSports as an occupation didn't really exist. I was in it purely because I liked it, for the sake of joy, and winning.'

Playing as 'cArn' – 'It stands for "carnage",' Sättermon says, 'which I thought was pretty cool when I was young' – he rose up the game's ranks until, just as he was considering withdrawing from the game to attend university, an offer came in to join an eSports team of no little ambition.

'I was planning to stop playing *Counter-Strike*, but then an ex-teammate of mine, when I was eighteen or nineteen, told me about an offer he'd had from Fnatic. He was putting together a team. I got the blessing from my family to be involved in that, and my original intent was to try it for a year, to see what happened. It was very much an adventure – nobody knew then what the pay cheques would be like come the end of each month. But while I had intended on being a pro-gamer for a year, I ended up doing it for seven, playing *Counter-Strike* across more than twenty-five countries.'

Sättermon was part of a Fnatic line-up that conquered all before them from 2006 until his retirement from *Counter-Strike* in 2012. In 2008 and 2009, he was bringing in prize money running to six figures, at a time when eSports prize pools were a far cry from today's sometimes tens of millions. With cArn at the helm, Fnatic's *CS* team was inarguably the greatest in the world. But while he was finally ready to lay down his rifle in 2012, Sättermon wasn't about to walk away from either Fnatic or eSports.

A Founding Father, and His Mother

In 2004, eSports was just beginning to realise its potential – the profile, the stars, the audiences, the sponsors and the money we see today. The World Cyber Games had debuted in 2000, attracting teams from seventeen different countries to compete in games including *Quake III Arena* and *FIFA 2000*, and four years later it left its home turf of

South Korea to stage a tournament in California, where players duked it out on *Halo, Counter-Strike: Condition Zero* and *Project Gotham Racing 2*. Major League Gaming was founded in the States in 2002, but didn't hold its first significant event until 2004's National Championship Finals in New York, featuring only *Halo* and *Super Smash Bros. Melee*. Baby steps were being taken, and the world was hardly watching in anticipation of a phenomenon blowing up. But in Britain, one man and his mother were thinking differently.

Sam Mathews was a keen gamer himself, with experience of competitive play, and saw the opportunity that the emerging array of global gaming tournaments presented anyone willing to invest time and money into stamping their brand on proceedings. He saw that this was a business that could be very beneficial not only on a personal level, but in terms of building a selection of teams to compete across a variety of titles.

With some sound advice from his mum, Anne, who co-founded the company as its financial director, Sam sold his car and invested £5,000 to establish Fnatic. In a 2010 Q&A on Fnatic's website, Anne remarked that her son shared her 'entrepreneur blood', adding: 'I . . . respect his ideas and ambitions . . . I needed another challenge, and this certainly has been one.' Sam's first order of business was forming a *Counter-Strike* team, which won its first high-profile tournament at 2005's CPL Singapore.

Speaking in a *VICE* documentary on eSports in 2015, Mathews attempted to describe Fnatic to an audience not necessarily familiar with the blossoming competitive gaming scene. 'Things like football are kind of limited in their scope,' he said, interviewed at the team's London HQ, 'whereas video gaming is not just one sport – it's like having a football team, and a tennis team, and a cricket team, all in one. And as a brand, and a company, that's exciting.'

He continued: 'eSports isn't just these geeks in a room, locked away. These guys are travelling around the world. They've got girls chasing them. And I can see these young kids becoming superstars and earning more money than I've earned.'

Mathews might be seeing a great return on his investment and vision today, but in the early days of Fnatic, not everything was smooth sailing. All but one member of its *Counter-Strike* team was let go in 2006, although that substantial shift in personnel paved the way for Sättermon's arrival. And as new teams were brought in – *World of Warcraft* in 2006 and *DotA* in 2007 – and competition spread to events around the globe, necessitating bases in overseas territories, Mathews was feeling the pressure to juggle more balls than his hands could reasonably catch. In a 2012 blog post on Fnatic's website, in which the co-founder answered a series of questions from the team's fans, he admitted that if he was to do it over today, things would be quite different.

> To get to tournaments, you needed sponsorship, [and] to get sponsors, you need to have a brand, a reputation and a following. They need to be able to trust you ...
>
> If I was to start a team this year, I would probably [only] focus on ... ONE region[, as] getting sponsors . . . interested in your team globally is very difficult. We struggled for many years as one of the least-sponsored teams compared to SK [Gaming, mousesports and more, because they had started as regional teams, and could gain sponsorship budget from the regional offices of Intel [and] Nvidia ... We always had to go global, which is the hardest part.

But aiming big at the beginning did pay off in other ways. With plenty of trusted staff and associates, including players and coaches, on the team's side, Fnatic was able to monitor everything that was happening in the professional gaming scene, while building a reputation as winners – primarily courtesy of its *CS 1.6* squad – which saw their fan base grow and grow. In 2010, Sättermon began to work closely with the team's management, 'encompassing the recruitment of other teams, discussing salaries with my colleagues, which was always a difficult topic being a player myself, and the overall operational side of things'. And he was one of the people at the organisation who was struck by just how huge a new MOBA was becoming.

The Allure of *League*

Sättermon recalls, '2010 was the year I came to London, to work at Fnatic. I basically just packed a bag and moved over there. I was working with Sam in a very small office. Well, it wasn't really an office at all, more a shared space where, on a lucky day, there'd be a spare seat for me, otherwise I'd have to work from home. It was nothing like the set-up we have now, with operations not only in London but also San Francisco, Kuala Lumpur, Berlin and Belgrade. I was still a pro-player, but I remember hearing about this new MOBA game that was blowing up in terms of viewership. *Counter-Strike* at that point would get something like thirty or forty thousand people watching concurrently, but *League of Legends*, ahead of its first World Championships, had over a hundred thousand. So that was an early eye-opener that this was a really big title in the making, and picking up a *League of Legends* team was definitely the right move. I was very supportive of us getting into the game.'

Rather than build a *League* team from the ground up, Fnatic did what it'd done with *DotA* and *WoW* before it and acquired one, effectively absorbing an existing, successful team into its roster. That team was myRevenge, based in Germany, which itself had been born via incorporating the oSk Gaming organisation. The deal went through in March of 2011, allowing for plenty of time ahead of *League*'s season one Championships, taking place in Sweden in June. The myRevenge team featured xPeke – aka Spanish AD carry Enrique Martínez, a player who'd go on to great success with Fnatic before leaving to form a European eSports organisation of his own, Origen – and Cyanide, a fine Finnish jungler otherwise known as Lauri Happonen. And at the centre of the new recruits was the captain of myRevenge, Tim Buysse, a Belgian whose gaming moniker was the somewhat unfortunate WetDreaM (perhaps it meant something else back home).

'Before *League of Legends*, I was just a casual gamer,' recalls Buysse, who's long retired from professional gaming. 'I always tried to be good at what I did, but I only tasted small success playing *Counter-Strike*. Nevertheless,

I did create a team, and we were one of the better ones in Belgium. That didn't mean much worldwide, but I really enjoyed the experience.

'Then, two of the guys from my *CS* team started playing *League of Legends*, when it was in its closed beta, and they got me an invite for it. I was immediately in love with it, and I was very soon playing it at a top level. Here's where I met Mike Petersen, known as Wickd, and we'd play and talk almost every day, and eventually went duo queue together. I got word of a tournament, and I wanted to create my own team, and that's when I found other people – Cyanide, xPeke, Mellisan [Peter Meisrimel], Shushei [Maciej Ratuszniak] and LaMiaZeaLoT [Manuel Mildenberger]. Some others tried out for the team, but they didn't make it. I taught the team that I had how to play together, as they were all outstanding already individually.

'We knew myRevenge had a shot at winning the first offline tournament we entered, but we never expected to go there, to the Intel Extreme Masters in Hanover, in March 2011, and do so without dropping a single game. It was there that we were approached by Fnatic, and as a long-time gamer I felt honoured to be asked by a team like that.'

Unfortunately for Buysse, his relationship with Fnatic was not to last. As he remembers it, 'Little did I know that joining an organisation like that would destroy everything I had built. It didn't take long before Fnatic tried to drop me. I left the team in May, to found the *LoL* community website Absolute Legends, and they ultimately went to the first season's Worlds in 2011 and won without me. But I was happy for them. I knew the team had potential, and that they would grow stronger. They've also made some good changes along the way, such as bringing in YellOwStaR, whose knowledge about the game has always been greater than almost any other player in Europe.'

Buysse's departure was felt by his now-former teammates, with Cyanide, via a Fnatic website-hosted Q&A, commenting: 'The grim thing about him leaving . . . was that he was the one to organize practice etc. So with him not being here, raging to us if we get to our computer too late [that] we have missed some practice hours.' As it turned out, those dropped sessions didn't prove decisive in Sweden.

'At the time of us winning the 2011 World Championship, it didn't feel like the achievement was anything legendary,' remembers Sättermon. 'We had no idea that this would be something that we'd still be talking about years later. The money for season one wasn't so high, even for eSports at the time. It just felt like one of many tournaments that year.'

'It was everyone's first try, not just ours,' says Finlay 'Quaye' Stewart, Fnatic's *League of Legends* team manager. 'No one else had won anything of that scale. The game hadn't really been established for very long. But with *DotA* being out for some years, *League of Legends* had no genuine MOBA competitors, so it got a huge player base really quickly. That definitely helped it reach the stage it's at today. It just made sense, at the very beginning, that this game was going to be one for the future.'

Reigning Supreme in Season One

While Fnatic won the first-ever *League of Legends* World Championship, the culmination of the Championship Series (the LCS, covering Europe and North America) featuring teams from Europe, North America and South East Asia, it so nearly went very wrong for them in the group phase of the finals, held during DreamHack in Jönköping, Sweden. Top-laner xPeke missed his flight north, and with substitute 'wewillfailer' – Belgian Bram De Winter, support for Nerv at the time of writing – standing in, Fnatic lost two of their three opening-round games. That saw them drawn against American outfit Counter Logic Gaming (CLG), one of the most established *League of*

Legends teams at the time (and today), in the first knock-out round, in a best-of-three tie. But with xPeke back in the starting five, Fnatic overcame their across-the-Pond rivals, setting up a semi-final contest against the team that'd topped their group with a perfect three wins from three, another (now-disbanded) American organisation, Epik Gamer.

Fnatic breezed past the team that'd beaten them in their previous encounter, two games to none, setting up a situation that might seem unusual to followers of traditional sports. In the final, they met against All authority (aAa), another team that'd beaten them in the group stage; and then, after aAa had dropped into, and returned from (guaranteeing them at least second spot), the loser's bracket of the tournament, they met again in the grand final. Their opponents were not to be taken lightly: amongst the five facing them was a rising talent by the name of Bora 'YellOwStaR' Kim, who'd join Fnatic two years later.

The decisive, title-determining game after a win each per team – netting the winners a cool $50,000 – started, as so many *League* games do, relatively sedately. Shushei drew first blood inside five minutes, having been the first to fall in Fnatic's previous tie, but no further champions had fallen by the fifteen-minute mark. And then Fnatic went up a gear, or three: xPeke took out YellOwStaR, sOAZ and Linak in quick succession in the middle of the map, earning a triple kill, while all the time the winners-in-waiting were farming more gold than their rivals. At half an hour, though, things were a lot closer: ten kills to eight in Fnatic's favour, with the same number of turrets destroyed. Each lane was being well controlled, with the teams balancing each other out fairly evenly. The fortieth minute saw Fnatic switch things up again, however, charging towards the aAa Nexus and claiming a huge number of kills, flipping that ratio to 21–11 in their favour. Three minutes later, after a brief fall back, Fnatic were all over the aAa base, and it was game over. GG indeed.

A Year of Change, and a Return to Greatness

The *League of Legends* World Championships grew into a monster the very next year. Instead of $50,000 going to the winners, season two's champions, Taipei Assassins, left Los Angeles with a life-changing $1 million to split between the team. With a total viewership of 8.2 million, including over a million concurrently, the October 2012 Worlds were the most-watched eSports event of all time, at the time. Fnatic failed to qualify for the finals – the only time in their history that they've not made the cut. Season two was something of

61

a transitional period for the team – as *League* got bigger, Fnatic's world-beaters began to fall apart. Shushei left in June and Mellisan in July, with new recruits failing to immediately gel alongside the remaining players into a winning formula.

The introduction of Martin Larsson, aka 'Rekkles', in November 2012 proved to be a catalyst for improvement – while too young, at sixteen, to play in the European *League* season proper, the LCS, he was able to take part in some late-year competitions. And what a difference he made: Fnatic went to November's DreamHack Winter competition perhaps expected to make up the numbers, and ran out winners. This achievement was followed by a second-place finish at the fifth IGN ProLeague finals in Las Vegas, where they were defeated by Chinese giants Team WE, and another runner-up result at the year-ending IEM Global Challenge in Cologne, at which South Korea's (double world champions to be) SK Telecom T1 emerged victorious. In between these silver finishes came a triumph at the 2012 THOR Open, held in Stockholm – quite the home-coming for the Swedish Rekkles.

First-place finishes in both the LCS Spring and Summer Playoffs in 2013 sealed Fnatic's reputation as the very best European *LoL* team at the time. The starting five was formidable, with xPeke and Cyanide in imperious form,

YellOwStaR's introduction bringing greater vision to the team's array of plays, former aAa man Paul 'sOAZ' Boyer dominating in the top lane, and Estonian Johannes 'puszu' Uibos filling in for the ineligible Rekkles as AD carry. October's Championship finals, again held in LA, promised another million-dollar first prize, and Fnatic qualified for it at a canter, going on to top their group with seven best-of-one wins and just a single defeat. North American champions and fan favourites Cloud9 stood between them and another semi-final.

As the sole remaining Americans in the tournament, there was great pressure on Cloud9 to maintain the local interest in proceedings; perhaps that pressure got to them, as Fnatic slaughtered their enemy in game one of three, wrecking their Nexus in the thirty-third minute. Cloud9 fought back to take a tighter second game, but the decider was as close to a whitewash as top-level *League* can witness, with Fnatic wrapping it up inside half an hour, the kill count a devastating 26–2 in their favour. The winners of season one were back, and how.

Fnatic couldn't go all the way in LA as they had in Sweden, though. Royal Club of China beat the final European team in the running 3–1 in the semis, ahead of losing to SK in the final, consigning Fnatic to a third/fourth-place finish – still an incredible result, and a real indicator that this was a team capable of competing, once again, with the very best in the world. And because of how *League* had exploded in scale since 2011, the prize money for a semi-finals finish was three times the winner's sum two years earlier.

Panic in Fnatic

Having looked so great in 2013, 2014 saw Fnatic's *League* team shaken down to its foundations, and a rebuilding process begin. Another first-place finish at the LCS Spring Playoffs was followed by a runners-up disappointment in the summer, and group stage elimination at the Worlds. Dissent was evident in the ranks, and unrest had taken hold of some players. Rekkles left in November to try his luck at LCS Summer Playoffs winners Alliance (which would almost immediately become Elements), and former myRevenge players xPeke and Cyanide departed in December to get Origen up and running. In January of 2015, sOAZ followed them out the door, also destined for Origen. That left only YellOwStaR, who found himself co-responsible for one hell of a recruitment drive while also dealing with doubts over his own abilities, given Fnatic's poor performance at the 2014 Worlds.

League was now bigger than ever: peak concurrent viewers for the 2014 Worlds had broken 11 million, while the final itself, contested between Samsung Galaxy White, the winners, and (the now rebranded Star Horn) Royal Club, defeated for a second time in consecutive finals, drew 40,000 fans to Seoul's Sangam Stadium, an arena previously used for the 2002 FIFA World Cup and the second-largest venue of its kind in South Korea. Fnatic could not be left behind. January 2015 saw a new head coach arrive, Luis 'Deilor' Sevilla, a man with a professional poker background and some *League* experience, but no previous LCS position. In the same month, four new players were welcomed into the Fnatic family – South Koreans Seung-hoon 'Huni' Heo and Kim 'Reignover' Ui-jin, Frenchman Pierre 'Steelback' Medjaldi and Dutch prodigy Fabian 'Febiven' Diepstraten. And it was a case of 'Crisis? What crisis?' when in April the new line-up took the LCS Spring Playoffs after finishing second in the regular season.

With Huni up top, Reignover in the jungle and Febiven down the middle, while YellOwStaR supported the returning Rekkles' AD carry role in the bottom lane (to make way, Steelback dropped to sub, before leaving for Odyssey Gaming in May), Fnatic won every game of the regular summer season, eighteen out of eighteen, an unprecedented feat yet to be repeated. They didn't drop one at all until the final of the Playoffs, where Origen took them all the way to a fifth game of five. It was quite the match-up, a mouth-watering tie where former teammates collided; but come the forty-third minute a relatively even contest swung wildly to Fnatic's side, as Huni nailed a triple kill and YellOwStaR went on a spree of his own, opening the Origen defences and leaving the Nexus exposed. Fnatic were going to the Worlds as Europe's number one seed.

Right Here, Right Now

Another third/fourth-place finish at 2015's Worlds was respectable, but it wasn't enough to keep the record-setting quintet of the summertime LCS season intact. In November 2015 both Huni and Reignover moved to the US to play for the newly founded Immortals, and in a surprise turn YellOwStaR went to the States too, to seek a new challenge at Team SoloMid (TSM). Into their roles came Germany's Lewis 'Noxiak' Felix (support), and another South Korean duo: Lee 'Spirit' Da-yun in the jungle, and top-laner Yeong-Jin Noh, aka 'Gamsu'.

'It was kind of like a package deal,' remembers Finlay Stewart, who joined as team manager in early 2016. 'So that's how it came about, really. Gamsu was such an anomaly when he came in, though, just so incredibly quiet.'

Gamsu wasn't riding high on confidence after a disappointing year with Team Dignitas in the American LCS, but he brought out the best in Spirit, and together the team finished second at March's ESL-organised Intel Extreme Masters tournament in Katowice. By this point Noxiak had left: 'I noticed pretty fast that Rekkles and I had very different ideas on how to play the [bottom] lane and the game in general,' he posted on Facebook on 12 February. 'We tried to balance our approaches but neither of us was . . . able to fix it. This resulted in a very low synergy between us.' In Poland, the team's recently recruited support substitute, Johan 'Klaj' Olsson, stepped in for the absent German, working well with his fellow countryman Rekkles as Fnatic – the tournament's only invited team from the European region – carved through Counter Logic Gaming before knocking out two Chinese teams, Qiao Gu Reapers and (the most excellently named) Royal Never Give Up. The 2015 world champions, SK Telecom T1, took the IEM final three games to nil, but given the player ins and outs that Fnatic had seen over the previous months, second place was not to be scoffed at.

The starting five of Spirit, Gamsu, Febiven, Rekkles and Klaj finished sixth in the regular spring LCS, just about qualifying for the Playoffs. A more than respectable third-place finish set them up for an optimistic 2016 summer season – which is where, at the time of writing, we find the team. There have been further changes to the roster, though. YellOwStaR returned to Fnatic in May, having expressed a desire to get back to Europe to TSM, who didn't stand in his way. Then Gamsu left the team in July, replaced by Polish top-laner Mateusz 'Kikis' Szkudlarek, who joined from summer league leaders G2 Esports. Two weeks after Kikis entered Fnatic's Berlin gaming house, the team confirmed the acquisition of an assistant coach to help Deilor and a new analyst, Nicholas 'NicoThePico' Korsgård and Wolfgang 'Wolle' Landes respectively. The summer LCS wrapped with Fnatic in fifth, meaning they'll play the fourth-finishing H2k-Gaming in the first round of the Summer Playoffs starting 13 August in Krakow, Poland. In August 2016, Deilor left Fnatic, with NicoThePico stepping up to head coach duties. 'It's a bittersweet feeling,' he wrote in an official statement, '[but] I will not take the trust he has put in me to waste.'

Bringing in Kikis met with positive press: the Score eSports reported that the top lane had been a weak spot for Fnatic all season, statistician Tim 'Magic' Sevenhuysen observing that the Pole had been steadily improving with G2, while adding that Gamsu's 'mistakes were usually more eye-catching than his successes'. The relationship between YellOwStaR and Rekkles continues to grow, too. As the only European LCS mainstay since season one, Fnatic's legendary status within the European *League* scene is assured. But the ingredients are there too for this team to get right back to the top. A roster in harmony, directed by a new coaching dynamic, all overseen by the icon that is cArn, a senior staffer who actually speaks the same language as those stepping out on stage week after week: it looks as though the stars are again aligning.

'We believe that, eventually, this will become much, much bigger than 90 per cent of world sports,' Sam Mathews told *VICE* in 2015. 'I really believe that.' And after everything that he's seen Fnatic achieve since 2004, are you going to doubt him?

5

In the House: Finlay Stewart on Managing Fnatic's Berlin Headquarters

*F*natic's League of Legends *team lives together in a special gaming house in Berlin – the city where all of the European LCS season games are played, at a television studio on the edge of the city. Here, team manager Finlay 'Quaye' Stewart provides an insight into what goes on in private, away from the glare of the stage lights and the gaze of the team's countless fans.*

BEFORE COMING here, I used to work in Fnatic's business development team. I was there for about six months, working with our current partners and reaching out to

new ones, focusing on league generation and deal broker-
ing, all this kind of stuff. I currently still manage a number
of accounts of partners, so I have multiple roles within
the organisation at the moment. But in December 2015
I moved into this role, managing the *League of Legends*
team, and here I am still.

Being the manager of Fnatic's *League of Legends* team
basically means I'm the one who is responsible for making
sure it runs like clockwork to benefit the overall atmosphere and team effectiveness. That basically means I am
the cleaner, the doorman, the bin man, all this kind of
stuff. I'm the guy who buys all of the food. I make sure
that the day-to-day stuff gets done, that everyone has what
they need to live. I suppose I'm something of a substitute
parent to some of the players in a way, too.

But I'm a lot more than that, too – I'm not just wip-
ing down a work surface once in a while and making sure
the fridge is stocked. I am also the players' agent, their
spokesperson; I organise all of their schedules and their
sponsorship meetings; all their interviews and press. I organise the acquisition of new players, I assist in the scouting
for new players, the running of the team and the subsid-
iary team – at times when we have a second team. It is a lot
of work because I have a lot of people to answer to, really,
across Riot Games and Fnatic, and of course the players

themselves. It can get intensive at times and quite stressful in the house, but at the same time it's good fun.

I live in the Berlin house with the players, so I don't have to worry about commuting to work – I wake up, usually around ten, and I'm already here. I suppose that's a luxury, but living in the house also means the players can ask anything of me, at almost any hour. Every day, someone will come and ask me something: 'Oh, Finlay, I need a new blind in my bedroom, because the light is coming through'; 'Finlay, hey, my eyes are hurting, can you go out and pick me up some eyewash?' And that can be fairly non-stop. Even at night, there's nothing stopping a player from knocking on my door with a problem: 'Hey, so, this just happened, and now my computer is broken. I need you to fix it because I don't know what to do.' I really have very little downtime, personally, because of needing to always be on the go, organising everything for the players, as and when they need it.

War and Peace

With all the players living in the same house, it's natural that friction happens, that frustrations arise – usually only because of a result, of how the team has performed recently. When it's a personal thing, I always encourage the player in question to speak to me, and I'll do whatever I can to sort it out. At the end of the day, I'm here to take as much pressure as I can off of their shoulders, so they can focus on what they're paid to do: to perform to the peak of their abilities, and be part of a winning team. Anything I can do to make them focus that bit harder on playing, to make them more comfortable and increase their performance level, it's part of my job.

We're always having meetings about the harmony of the house – it's important to address issues that come up, either in a group or on a one-on-one basis. Whenever a mediator is required, we'll ensure that third person is there to help out. We deal with every issue in a professional way – everyone in the house is a professional and they're paid to work together. However, I appreciate that it can be hard for them to understand how to cooperate with one another, sometimes, especially early on, because none of these guys have worked in an office environment. When you do, and someone, an individual, is having problems, you can't simply drop whatever you're doing – it's tough shit, basically, because you have to get on with it and do your job.

In *League*, you see teams and players who don't get along, personally, but those teams can still win because they do their job: they work together and play the game. That said, it's better that the players in a team are friends – having that extra bond between them means that problems that come up are dealt with easier, and the individuals can be more open with each other, talking through whatever is bothering them as friends.

If anyone does anything that affects the harmony of the household, I tend to take them aside, or sometimes Luis will, or Bora, and let them know how their actions have impacted on other people. Usually they agree, and you'll hear: 'I shouldn't have done that.' But every little upset improves the overall atmosphere, because the players here get better with talking things through, the more these situations come up. It's just like the game: the more you practise, the better you become, and if something you're doing isn't working for the best for everyone, you learn not to do it.

I never shout at anyone in the house. I don't think I've ever had to. I get annoyed sometimes, and I raise my voice, but I never get angry. The guys know what they have to do, and no one is a complete slob or idiot.

Free Time and Fan Management

We usually have Saturday as a day off and, if I'm honest, a few of us can be pretty hungover because of whatever we got up to the night before. It's important to take time out from the game. Some Fridays can be quite sedate – we'll go out to the cinema, or some players will go out for a meal. We do go to restaurants as a team, but a lot of what goes on comes down to how the players are feeling. Some just stay inside and play more *League* on their day off.

When it comes to fans, I think all of the players in the team are comfortable with dealing with them, meeting them after games, signing autographs and so on. That said, it definitely affected Febiven when he started here. He was very nervous, and awkward all of the time. Nowadays he's pretty famous, and just like the other players he has so many fans. Actually, he's become quite demanding, quite the opposite from the shy guy he was when beginning his career as a newbie. One area he maybe still struggles in is feedback – he'll take comments on how he's been playing as personal criticism, when we're all just trying to help him. He thinks we're attacking him, when really we're just trying to make everything better for him, and the team. But I think that's quite normal for young guys, anyway – when you're less mature, you simply don't handle any criticism well.

Wherever the players go, and whoever they speak to on their time off, we always keep the location of the house a secret when meeting new people. If it was public knowledge we would constantly have people waiting for us outside – I'm not sure how many, exactly, but I could imagine double digits over the course of an average week. That could disrupt our preparation, especially when leaving for matches in the LCS. I also have a rule about girls: only girlfriends are allowed in the house. No player can bring back, for want of a better word, a random for the night. If this girl is a big fan of the team, what's to stop her sharing the location with people on Twitter? Honestly, if that got out there it'd be a real problem – we'd simply have so many people milling around, outside the house.

Jokers in the Pack

Everyone's personality in the team is different. I think Febiven and Spirit are the jokers in the house – they're just funny individuals, who find a lot of things a laugh, and that's infectious. They don't go out of their way to play pranks on the others guys, but you can guarantee that if something funny's going on, it's usually one of those two who started it. Then again, I've been known to pull a prank or two, to keep things lively.

When it comes to someone with the strictest routine, that's Bora, YellOwStaR, definitely. So he wakes up at like seven o'clock and goes to the gym, comes back, has coffee and a protein shake. Every day is the same. He goes to sleep at ten or eleven o'clock. Martin, Rekkles, is very similar – he gets up not quite that early, but maybe heads to the gym at around nine o'clock, and he goes to bed early too. Around the time of the last Split, the Spring Split, Gamsu and Spirit would be staying up until 4 or 5 a.m., and waking up after midday – the opposite of the European players. We've been trying hard to get everyone on the same sort of routine, though.

We have two bathrooms in the house, and they're always in use – the guys take a long time to get themselves ready before going to play, or heading out into town. Rekkles and Fabian, Febiven, they both take a really long time, probably about the same amount. But then Spirit can be in there a while too, as was Gamsu. The only guy who's ready fast is Bora. It's not as if he doesn't care about how he looks at all, but he's got short hair and he doesn't take ages styling it. He's just ready, and then he goes. Gamsu used to spend a long time blow-drying his hair, and the others are always looking in the mirror, checking their hair, making sure their clothes are all right, that kind of thing. Of course, then they go and put headphones on, so I'm not always sure why they spend so long on their hair before going on stage.

A few of the guys have been known to play other games in the house, like *Rocket League* and *Overwatch*, but for the most part everyone exclusively focuses on *League*. We have a TV, and sometimes we gather around it with ice cream – there's a Häagen-Dazs cafe close to the house – but the players don't watch a lot of television. Box sets can prove popular, and like everyone in the world, we have our share of *Game of Thrones* fans in the house. We *always* watch the episodes on the day they come out, so that not knowing what happens doesn't affect anyone's focus on the games to come. I'm guilty of watching it when I should be working, keeping it open in a window on my computer. But then, none of us wants the show spoiled for us – and we're online so much, that's a real danger. Somehow, we need to get Fnatic into Westeros.

6

Inside the *League of Legends* World Championships

There is no greater honour, no higher achievement, in competitive *League of Legends* than to be the World Champions, claiming the Summoner's Cup for yourself at the end of an intense season. Fnatic was the first team to reach this summit, winning in 2011, at DreamHack Summer, the year before the enormous 32-kilogram trophy's introduction. 'I think it's so big that the whole team of five can lift it at the same time,' says YellOwStaR, on the losing side of the 2011 final. 'As a competitor, though, that's all you're looking at, *the trophy*. You want to achieve that as a player, and be part of the best team, and you want to have deserved it.'

League's modest debut season was not to be repeated in 2012: the World Championship finals were held in Los Angeles with a million-dollar top prize – and of course that cup – to the winners. That team was Taipei Assassins, now called J Gaming after a buyout by Taiwanese musician and actor Jay Chou. Their win kick-started a period of Eastern dominance, with 2013's title, again decided in LA, going to South Korea's SK Telecom T1. Thirty-two million people streamed their climactic contest against China's Royal Club – more people than tuned into 2013's NBA Finals and baseball's World Series of the same year. And for 2014, *League* was going bigger still – this time in the proverbial flesh.

Stadium Gaming

The grand final of 2014 wasn't in an arena, a conference centre or some other specialist events space with four walls and a roof to keep the heat and the hype in. Riot went all out like never before, hosting the best-of-five finish to season four in Seoul's Sangam Stadium, aka the Seoul World Cup Stadium. Today the venue can hold 66,000 fans for football matches, such as the 2013 AFC Champion's League final and the national team's home ties. For *League*'s biggest-ever live occasion, every possible stop was yanked from its resting place. The format of the event meant that not every seat in the house could be occupied, but a massive 40,000 fans crowded into the stadium to see South Korean local favourites Samsung White and China's Star Horn Royal Club click off against each other.

'Even though you know the capacity, how many people are coming and everything, I didn't expect what I saw,' remembers Rhys James, producer/director of *VICE*'s 2015 eSports documentary, aka *The Celebrity Millionaires of Competitive Gaming*. He was shooting in Seoul for the film, soaking in the atmosphere, observing all he could. 'People were *really* excited. The scale of it all, the production, was on a level I'd not experienced at many stadium rock shows, or at a lot of traditional sports. It's not exactly an everyday thing to see flamethrowers at a rugby match – but what I saw in Seoul was like the Super Bowl, in terms of the attention to detail that was going on. It was cherry-picking all of these elements from elsewhere. In ice hockey, you have the big foam fingers, and the light-up wristbands are something I know they've had at Coldplay concerts.'

James saw a side of gaming he'd never seen before, where people proficient in playing, to say the least, weren't simply chasing high scores and leaderboard bragging rights. They were cast as bona-fide megastars, celebrities walking among their flock, swallowed by the throng at their every turn.

'I saw people who were completely obsessed with some of the teams. In Korea, a lot of people were freaking out over the American team Cloud9, and their player Hai [Lam]. He got totally mobbed, and he attracted a lot of attention from the cosplayers and dancers at the event. He was surrounded by these absolute babes, if I'm honest, who were totally focused on him and nobody else, not even the game itself.

'There are clearly teams out there that are very happy to pursue that players-as-celebrities route, who recognise their value to the brand. You see that a lot with the European and American teams – Fnatic has a rabid fan base because of how they've marketed themselves, for example. The Korean and Chinese players that I saw in Seoul seemed a lot more serious, that bit more private when it came to meeting fans. But they all have their character names, their gamertags, which does give them this warrior-like identity, this celebrity status, however they are in person.

'Nevertheless, people were always hyped to meet the players. Before we went to Seoul, we filmed in Germany, at the LCS qualifiers at Gamescom. It was there that I saw someone had put up a sign that said, "Rekkles Can Wreck

Me." This was by young girls, and I suppose that was a bit distressing, actually. But it shows you that people really are *obsessed* with these players. We saw xPeke called "SexPeke" at that event too.'

Reporting at the time for the BBC News website, Stephen Evans wrote of the 2014 final: '[This] may only have been an online game – or e-sport, as the players and promoters prefer to call it – but it had all the feel of any traditional major sporting drama.' He met fans rushing into the stadium, one of whom told him, when asked if this was all a little nerdy: 'I don't think so. Right now, this is mainstream. Look at all these people here.'

Champions and 'Warriors'

Another sign that this was no niche event was the booking of Imagine Dragons to perform at the grand final. The Las Vegas rock band already had a stateside number one album under their collective belt in the shape of 2012's *Night Visions*, had won both Grammy Awards and American Music Awards for said debut collection, and had made appearances on several television shows. To the band, the world of eSports was alien, but exciting – something fresh to their promotional cycle, and bringing with it a potentially massive new audience. Riot reached out to them, and a creative collaboration was born with 'Warriors', a song recorded specially for the 2014 *League* Worlds and showcased within the Sangam Stadium.

'It was an amazing experience,' bassist Ben McKee told the *Korea Times*' website in June 2015, reflecting on 'Warriors' and the Worlds. '"Warriors" was a really cool collaborative process, and we created different versions of the song. Being able to play at the *League of Legends* Championship last year allowed us our first opportunity to come over to Korea and play for our fans.' The country left an impression on McKee – or rather, on his stomach: 'When I came back home, I actually went out to go get some bibimbap [a Korean rice dish] because I was still craving it. But the kimchi [fermented vegetables] they served in Korean restaurants in Las Vegas was so wrong. I immediately missed Korea and we just can't wait to come back. We all had a great time there.'

'Warriors' was an instant hit with *League* fans, with comments on its high-budget animated video's posting to leagueoflegends.com ranging from 'the goosebumps are real' to 'THE FEELS!!!!' (yes, with that many exclamation marks). It's only had 54 million views on YouTube, no big deal. At the Worlds themselves, backed by an orchestra and introduced (and accompanied) by the pounding of a legion of taiko drums, the song crackled into the Seoul air, met by row upon row of fans bearing light-up thundersticks. At the big finish, fireworks popped and the crowd erupted: just like that Super Bowl feeling. After Samsung White got their hands on the Summoner's Cup, the band returned for a run through more of their hit songs, like 'On Top of the World' and 'Radioactive', as the triumphant players high-fived their fans down at the front. This was so much more than just a video game now; this was top-tier entertainment on a level with anything other mediums could muster.

Not that everything in Seoul was all fire and brimstone, the money on show, bursting into colour, for all to see. 'They had these two compères, who were there to keep the crowd hyped, and they had loads of people throwing out buckets of swag,' James remembers. 'To be honest, a lot of the kids there seemed more excited about the swag than the games themselves. It was funny to see people so excited about what is just promotional stuff, really, free advertising – but that was tiding them over until the games began.

'I'm pretty sure Riot makes a loss putting that kind of show on,' James muses – and to some extent he's right. In 2013, it was revealed that the LCS doesn't turn a profit for Riot. 'It's a significant investment that we're not making money from,' Riot's eSports head, Dustin Beck, told PCGamesN at that year's Gamescom. 'It's an investment into the game, for our fans, just like we'd invest in any other feature within the game. It's a worthwhile thing for us to do because it's such a high quality, engaging experience.' It's fortunate, then, that *League* has been such a success at encouraging microtransaction activity – that's all of those new skins and champions that fans have been buying up while *playing* the game for free. Between January and September 2014, the game brought in $964 million, adding up to over a billion dollars by the end of the year, and in 2015 the game was making Riot around $31 every second. Whatever the spend on the season-ending celebration of competitive *League*, then, there's little worry right now of the funds drying up.

European Tour

The 2015 Worlds left the East behind and, for the first time since 2011, they were staged in Europe, with the quarter-finals – featuring teams not only from the North American and European LCS leagues, South Korea's finest and Chinese heavyweights, but also wildcard outfits from Chile and Turkey – held across four days at London's Wembley Arena. The BBC made the almost unprecedented move of covering the last eight in a fully committed fashion, producing a series of introductory videos for total newcomers to the game and taking the same scale of crew to Wembley as they would to a major sporting event.

'It was the BBC's first foray into covering eSports, and it was a co-production between [digital channel] BBC Three and BBC Sport,' remembers the BBC's host for the 2015 Worlds, Julia Hardy. 'It was full-on BBC Sport in terms of production, which was really nice to see. It wasn't so much of a stretch from what Riot do themselves in terms of pre-sentation, because what they do is incredibly professional, but it was really nice to see the BBC go in for eSports in such a committed way.

'What they did really well was pitch the event to people who weren't already really into *League*. Naturally, if you were, you were probably watching the Riot stream, as that was catered to you. The BBC was aware, going into its coverage, that it couldn't assume that viewers would have all the necessary knowledge. A lot of people know about *League*, but they don't really *understand* it. So they decided to come from the standpoint of trying to educate people, as they were learning themselves, really.

'So, there were a lot of little packages made up for the web, which helped newcomers get into the basics. Having those to seed the show meant that anyone who was totally green before got a head start for understanding what was actually happening in the matches. It helped people feel prepped.

And the BBC brought in a lot of the right people – some great shoutcasters, good behind-the-scenes people to do the live blogging. They got a lot of people who were real specialists in their fields, who were able to explain things in a way that wasn't too jargony. And that was a great way to help people understand.'

For four straight days, *League* fans assembled at Wembley, as the European contenders channelled the local support to overcome their opponents. Both Fnatic and Origen won their quarter-final matches convincingly, against EDward Gaming and Flash Wolves respectively, two teams from the Chinese Pro League. But eSports is rarely like traditional equivalents – fans will come to support a team and its players, of course, but they'll also be quick to vociferously appreciate a fine play in motion, whoever is pulling it off.

'There are definitely crowds rooting for Fnatic over in Europe over other teams in the same league,' says Matt Porter, an eSports journalist for outlets including IGN and *PC Gamer*. 'The Wembley crowd was going mad for the European teams. But *League* really isn't like following football, or something like that. With a sport like football, you'll usually support the team that plays where you're from; but in eSports, it's more about the personalities, and sometimes even following them from team to team.'

'But a lot of people were supporting the teams from outside of Europe too,' says Hardy. 'Everyone was just super excited to be there, watching the competition, on stage and not on a screen at home. Everyone was so hyped, and going insane for everything. People have their teams, of course, but everyone would cheer when they saw a good play, as opposed to just cheering on "their guy".'

Establishment Endorsement

'From the BBC's point of view, they'd heard about the numbers that would watch online, and they'd seen the footage from Korea, from the 2014 World Championship final,' Hardy recounts. 'But seeing people coming from BBC Sport be surprised at the level of enthusiasm for games, something that isn't what they understand to be competitive, or a sport, was a real eye-opener. They knew all about it already; but to actually be there and hear the crowd, and feel the energy and excitement, I think they were gobsmacked and blown away. It's all very well seeing a bunch of stats on paper, but to actually feel it and experience it live is something else.'

League of Legends fans are used to streaming the action from key events online, so for them, it's not like the presence of the BBC at Wembley was anything to get excited about. But what it represented, in a wider sense, was recognition from a centre-mainstream broadcaster that eSports was not an underground phenomenon. This was happening now, and was going to continue happening for the foreseeable. And like any company wanting an advantage over competitors – and in the BBC's case, a Royal Charter to adhere to – getting in with a bang set a powerful precedent.

'The BBC were a little tentative, a little worried about the reaction,' Hardy says. 'But the response to our coverage was so overwhelmingly positive, because people could see the potential for covering this more in the future. Having this at Wembley, with so many people going crazy, it was a perfect time for the BBC's first eSports event.

'At the end of the day, without the BBC even touching it, *League* is monstrously successful, overwhelmingly popular. They don't need the BBC to do anything. But what was nice was, if you're a gamer who feels like they've been ignored by the mainstream media for as long as you can remember, to have someone like the BBC step forward and say, "We respect this, and we want to learn more and we want to produce content around this thing that you're passionate about," it's a seal of approval from somewhere you never expected. Not really from "the establishment", but from more traditional media, which has never really happened before. Gaming has always been this little thing – we just get on with it, and we do our thing, and occasionally it seeps over into the mainstream but generally speaking it tends to stay over here. So for the BBC to be involved, it shows that eSports has arrived; that this is the starting point of it getting even bigger, and going to that next level.'

Being a public face, and font of information, for the Worlds is a tough gig too. Speaking to Engadget in October 2015, *League* shoutcaster Trevor Henry, aka 'Quickshot', explained that it's a demanding time for commentators and pundits, just as it is for the players themselves:

> You can't count the hours . . . What goes into Worlds is a bigger and more intense version of my regular work . . . [W]e've got a very big production team behind the camera that a lot of people don't know about . . . producers, directors, scriptwriters, graphics guys, video guys, editors, journalists, statisticians . . . our weekly prep and show prep involves touching base with [all] of them. What story do we feel is the most important? Which players do we want to look deeper at? . . .
>
> [W]e are literally required to talk for five, six hours a day. There's a whole lot that goes on off-air that

then leads up to what is, relatively speaking, a short, one-off broadcast per day.

Continental Drift

Four teams left London with their eyes still on the prize: Fnatic and Origen, joined by South Korean pair KOO Tigers and 2013's champions SK Telecom T1. The next destination was the Expo in Brussels, Belgium, for two days of what promised to be intense competition. But despite being 'home' favourites, plying their trade in the Berlin-centred EU LCS, neither one of the two European teams could take a game off their opponents. Fnatic went down 3–0 against KOO, while the same scoreline saw Origen bounced from the competition.

'It was a disappointment that none of the European teams made the actual final,' says Matt Porter. 'That Origen and Fnatic were in the semis at all was slightly against the odds, but once they were there, it was hoped that one of them could progress. It would have been a lot more exciting for local fans had one of the teams that actually plays in Berlin, for their league games, made it to the final there. But then, it's always good to see the best playing against the best, even if they're from a different region. And I think it's safe to say that the best two teams in the world, in 2015, were the two that got to the final. SK didn't lose a single game until the final itself, so they were definitely the favourites before the tournament had reached Germany. It was great to see Fnatic do so well, but I don't think anyone on the team that year would have argued against KOO and SK being the very best.

'Despite the absence of a European team, the crowd in the Mercedes-Benz Arena was really up for it,' Porter continues. 'The most exciting part of the final was when KOO Tigers unexpectedly took a game off SKT, which took it to game four. The crowd *really* got going then, because they were rooting for the underdogs.

'People began showing up hours ahead of the games starting. You'd see people in cosplay, and hundreds of people congregating, meeting up, checking out stores and art exhibitions. The staging of the games themselves was amazing. They had all these moving LEDs, and the players' faces coming up, and all the champions they were playing as next to them on the stage. They were playing in a kind of circular arena, which helped a little too. Usually in eSports you have the two teams looking out to the audience; but here they were looking at each other, which added to the drama of it all.'

There was some disappointment amongst *League*'s fan base that the 2015 Worlds had not been held in a stadium the size of what they'd witnessed in Seoul. But it'd been Riot's intention to scale the final rounds down a little, and increase the atmosphere, and the noise, inside each venue. The 17,000-capacity Mercedes-Benz Arena is used for basketball and ice hockey matches, among other things, and, says Porter: '[Riot] said, at a press conference I attended, that they wanted a tighter atmosphere, more like a basketball match.'

American Dreams and Eternal Memories

Once all the regional qualifying matters are decided, the 2016 World Championship is again a touring affair, crossing the Atlantic from Europe to America once again. The group stage, where sixteen teams will compete, will play out at San Francisco's Bill Graham Civic Auditorium over two weekends at the end of September and the beginning of October. From there, it's on to the Chicago Theatre, in the Windy City itself, to cut eight teams down to four. The world-famous Madison Square Garden, which can hold close to 20,000 people, is the scene for the semis, and then the final returns to Los Angeles: 29 October, the Staples Center – be there, or be online with the action flowing directly to your screen of choice. 'I'm not sure it gets much bigger than that' is Porter's thought on the Worlds' climax for 2016.

Whatever the outcome of the 2016 Worlds, all who compete will take away memories to last a lifetime, be they ones to cherish or the kind to banish to the very darkest corner of one's grey matter. The Worlds has always been a place for magical moments that stand out in fans' own remembering of the winners and runners-up. Those who watched season two closely won't forget the amazing group-stage form of South Korean team NaJin Sword's top-laner MaKNooN, who dominated the opposition with incredibly aggressive plays. Taipei Assassins' season two win came, while not entirely out of the blue, certainly against form, as going into that year's Worlds all eyes were on rising Russians Moscow Five – who'd blazed a trail through the likes of CLG Europe and SK Gaming – and now-disbanded South Korean contenders Azubu Frost. Yet the eventual winners defeated both of them on their way to claiming the Summoner's Cup.

Faker versus Cool was the talk of the 2013 Worlds, as the two celebrated, assassin-using mid-laners came up against each other when SKT took on China's OMG in the group phase. The South Koreans took it in the end, but the mid-laners' one-on-one encounters were explosive sideshows to the wider significance of the game on the group's final standings. In the same year, Europeans Gambit Gaming managed to squeeze the much-tipped South Koreans

Samsung Galaxy Ozone out of a top-two group-phase finish – the last time a South Korean outfit didn't make it into the quarter-finals. And of course, Fnatic's run to the semis in 2015 was an incredible, indelible memory for all involved, especially the players. 'Our mindset was simply: we want to win the World Championship,' YellOwStaR remembers, acknowledging that even though the team fell just before the final, they can all feel proud of their achievement. It wasn't to be in 2015, but the future is there for the taking, if a team wants it enough.

And for the fans, those watching at home and at the arenas themselves, the Worlds will always be the pinnacle of the competitive scene – a must-not-miss series of games that will continue to bring more spectators and casual players alike into *League*. 'For me, personally, I get a real buzz off people being really passionate about stuff,' says Julia Hardy. 'It's so infectious; it's like a drug, almost. You can't help but get swept away when everyone's so excited – and that gets even more people into this. When you're at the games, in person, you see all the pitfalls of them, all the highs and the lows. You have thousands and thousands of people around you, shouting and screaming – and you've got to be pretty dead inside to not get swept up in that, and enjoy the experience of seeing this live.'

7

What Makes, and Breaks, a Professional *League of Legends* Player

Every professional gamer aims to reach the highest highs available to them in their discipline of choice. Usually, this means claiming the world championship in that game. Few, though, ever achieve that glory, and this affects players in different ways. Some will persist with their training, putting in countless hours, going over the mechanical and cultural developments of their particular game. You only need to spend an hour in any gaming house to see this commitment: eyes on the screen, attention fully focused, everything else in the world reduced to a blurry insignificance. But just as with traditional sports, some competitors in eSports have turned to illegal avenues to make their time in the scene more profitable.

From match-fixing to doping scandals, eSports has reached a level of maturity where its darker side has made headlines around the world. Its rapid development, with tens of global tournaments turning into hundreds in the shortest amount of time, and rising prize pools – *DotA 2*'s International has seen its first-place prize go from $1 million in 2011 to over $6.5 million in 2015, thanks to player contributions – has put untold pressure on young men to be a success however they can, regardless of their performances on stage and screen.

In late 2015 and early 2016, the competitive *StarCraft II* scene was rocked by several match-fixing revelations, which included former world champion Hyun 'Life' Lee, one of the game's all-time legends, throwing two 2015 matches for seven times the top prize of the tournament in question. He was subsequently arrested, prosecuted and, in July 2016, sentenced to a suspended eighteen months in prison for his crimes. He also received a fine amounting to the same sum he'd been given for losing the matches in question, 70,000,000 South Korean won – around £48,000, or $63,000.

'I think some people might come to eSports for the money, but I wouldn't recommend it' is YellOwStaR's take on the motivating factor for playing at the highest level. 'You can see the difference between those who are in it because they think they can make money, and those who are in it to win – who will make money anyway, because they're winning. Naturally, when you perform well, you'll get to the better teams, and money will come to you. So I think it's the wrong approach to come to eSports for the money. That's not going to last long.'

A Broken Promise

In early 2014, *League of Legends* was hit by a match-fixing drama of its own, with tragic repercussions. The Korea eSports Association, the KeSPA, looked into allegations made by ahq e-Sports Club Korea's AD carry Cheon Min-Ki, aka 'Promise', that the team was being coerced by its manager, Noh Dae Chu, to throw matches on purpose. Indeed, Promise's accusation went further: he posted on internet forums that the whole team was set up for such activity, specifically created to facilitate illegal betting.

'Our manager . . . lied to us,' Promise, who'd moved to ahq from NaJin Sword, wrote on the Inven.co.kr forum. '[He] took out a loan to pay for our housing, living expenses, computers, even our salaries [rather than actually having ahq's sponsorship]. He was planning on placing illegal bets on eSports games and fixing them to win back the borrowed money and make a profit.'

The KeSPA immediately contacted Promise's ahq teammates to learn more. They could not, however, speak to Promise himself as, shortly after posting the allegations, he attempted suicide by falling from the rooftop of a twelve-storey building. He'd telegraphed his intention in the Inven post, writing: 'I am sorry for all of this, and I can't tell you everything, but I'm leaving now as I can't deal with this anymore.' He survived only because he landed in a recycling area, his impact cushioned by a plastic bin lid. Nevertheless, he broke several bones including an arm, a leg and his jaw, and ended up in a coma. Doctors spent eleven hours working on his injuries, and the gaming community rallied to his cause, raising $53,000 towards his medical bills.

Promise had been gaming since he was three years old. He was devoted to *League*, and to being a professional gamer, to improve his way of life – coming from a poor family, he'd survived on instant noodles and cheap cans of coffee for too long. To him, this career was everything, and to have someone skew it towards an entirely different kind of gain, against the ethics of competition, was more than he could handle.

'[The manager] was a fraudster, who was very good at speaking,' a recovered Promise told *VICE*, in their 2015 eSports documentary. 'He wanted us to fix a few matches. I didn't want to do it. But if I didn't do it, they said there wouldn't be a future for me as a professional player. I couldn't get on with my life because of the scandal, which is why I attempted suicide.'

The KeSPA concluded that only Promise was involved in the ahq match-fixing, and that his teammates were not guilty of deliberately playing to lose. Promise has not played competitively since his recovery, but is at least able to enjoy gaming again – in 2015, he tweeted his excitement for the E3-announced *Final Fantasy VII* remake, and would stream gameplay from titles totally unconnected with *League*, like first-person shooter *Metro Redux*, via Twitch.

Knowing Right from Wrong

Promise's case is an extreme example of the way that a pro-gamer's career can break down in ways they never could have expected. For some, like Tim Buysse, the internal relationships were never quite so fraught as what went on at ahq, but when he left Fnatic ahead of the 2011 Worlds it was entirely down to a disconnect between employee and organisation, something that can happen in any profession, and eSports is no different.

'I left the game because of all the season one drama,' he says. 'I tried to continue playing for a period after I left Fnatic, at SK Gaming, but pretty much the same happened there. So I formed Absolute Legends with Wickd [Mike Petersen], and then they got merged into Counter Logic Gaming, and that was enough for me. I had had enough of all this immature behaviour with no respect for other human beings that I chose to quit everything around game and focus on real life.

'I never look back and think about "what if", because I am not the kind of person. If you think every time about "what if", then you will get depressed or frustrated sooner or later. Nowadays I don't talk to any of my former teammates, except Mellisan sometimes. But I have other friends from my *League* days, who I still see, so I'm thankful for that, and that's why I'll never forget or regret my time playing *League*.'

From a team's perspective, it's essential – however disappointing it is for the individuals affected – that the right balance is struck in the starting five, and that there's harmony in all the right places. Fnatic's *League of Legends* head coach from the start of 2015 to the summer of 2016, Luis 'Deilor' Sevilla, accepts, though, that it's not easy to find the correct recipe for positive results right from the get-go:

'Seeing who is going to come big, or who is going to choke, at key moments in a game, that's not easy. Sometimes you really cannot predict that. I've seen players who are really shy when they're around you, around the rest of the team, perform really strongly when it counts; and the opposite can be true, too, where someone is very outgoing in person, but they don't bring that to the game. There's no clear pattern there. But I do see how the best players are also the ones that know when to be hard on themselves – because if you're not able to be critical of yourself, you're not going to improve at the speed that this game demands. That is really easy to see. We've had an academy team here before, and it was easy to see, after just two weeks of training, which players were not cut out to make it at the top level.

'I've spent a lot of time in basketball, and coaches there will teach you a little about shooting, a little about dribbling, but really a little amount of technique. That comes through exercises, practice, repetition. The main emphasis is always on how that player can fit into the team. So I will tap the knowledge of every player, and feed that back into the overall team experience, because that is a massive amount of knowledge, and it's very specialised. The players, they often have blinkers on when it comes to what they know and what they do in a game. The blinkers are necessary, because of the role each player has. Their role is super specialised. It's on me to be able to remove these blinkers from time to time in order to get the very best out of the five guys.'

Disruptive Elements

When one of said five guys isn't pulling their weight, doesn't quite fit the meta or how the organisation sees it at least, or is at odds personally with those around him, it's rare that a team will exhibit too much patience in order to resolve the conflict. One only need look at the team history of most players competing in the LCS to see that regularly transferring between organisations is at the very heart of the professional game. At Fnatic, however, the emphasis is always on peaceful resolution rather than player replacement.

'I think we're very diplomatic,' says Fnatic CGO Patrik Sättermon. 'We look for ways to resolve problems within the team we have. We might consider swapping players around within a certain game, but that doesn't always make sense, because it's a smaller jump between being a sniper and a support player in *CS:GO* [*Counter-Strike:*

Global Offensive] compared to moving from a top-laner to the middle lane in *League*. But we always try to understand things, and be open about issues. We try to motivate players to find the changes we need. Losing one big tournament, or being unsuccessful for three to six months at a time, that's not something that means we're automatically going to kick people out.

'And we've seen that in the past – we've exhibited a lot of patience with our *CS:GO* team, which wasn't having the greatest time in 2013. But we stuck to our values and worked hard, and today the team is doing really well for itself. I had a great gut feeling that'd happen. We have a better approach to internal issues than other teams, I think, and that's based on a lot of understanding. We're never going to just pay people a lot of money and demand that they win – that won't get you a lot of results.'

At other LCS teams, however, one player's actions have left management with no choice but to show him the door. 'This is just one example out of hundreds, I'm sure,' says Fnatic's *League* manager, Finlay Stewart, 'but back at the start of the 2016 summer season, we saw Forg1ven [Greek AD carry Konstantinos Tzortziou] join Origen, and then leave almost straight away.' (He tweeted on 9 July 2016: 'I didnt wake up one day and left them, i got removed.')

'He's one of these players that jumps from team to team, but who always fought to be the best player in his role – and skill-wise he certainly is one of the best. But his attitude and personality was so bad that a team could never make it work with him on their roster, because he would just destroy the team from the inside.

'Historically, he's been good enough to carry some games completely, but that didn't make up for the fact that he would be abusing his teammates, calling them out and having just a terrible attitude. So even this player, who is incredibly skilled, doesn't cut it because he's not a *team* player. This is a team game and at the end of the day you need players that are skilled, of course, but also that gel together.'

Forg1ven's professional record certainly has its black marks, foremost amongst them a $1,000 fine from Riot in 2014 for, as PCGamesN reported at the time, 'in-game harassment, verbal abuse and . . . "toxicity"'. Riot's eSports manager at the time, Nick Allen, commented:

Tzortziou has continued to consistently engage in behaviour which violates the letter and spirit of the Summoner's Code [the set of rules and recommen- dations, that players both professional and casual are asked to abide by]. His tendency to engage in verbal abuse, insults and offensive behaviour is unacceptable for any player . . . This behaviour is especially harmful in a high-profile eSports competitor who should lead the community by example.

Second chances are far from unheard of, though, and Forg1ven plays in the LCS today, for H2k. In April 2015, a *League* player who'd not only been fined but also banned from the game completely was offered an olive branch by Riot. Nicolaj Jensen, who previously played under the gamertag of 'Incarnati0n' but these days appears as simply 'Jensen', saw a perma-ban imposed in January 2013 lifted, allowing him to return to action – as of the summer of 2016, the Danish mid-laner is slowly stepping out of Hai Du Lam's shadow at Cloud9. His ban came about because of highly toxic behaviour when playing solo queue, as well as allegedly DDoSing (distributed denial-of-service) opponents. His reprieve represented the first time Riot had ever lifted such a ban.

Riot reported, in lifting Jensen's ban, that the player had 'continued to demonstrate behaviour in game that is well above the normal standards', and that 'there have been no serious offenses or violations of the letter or the spirit of the Summoner Code'. The verdict: he was allowed to compete once more, and in July 2016 Jensen scored a pentakill on stage for the first time, against Apex Gaming in the NA LCS Summer Split, causing the crowd to go wild. Comeback completed.

Saying Hello, Saying Goodbye

But changes in a player's behaviour are something that all teams must look out for, not only due to pressure being put upon them to remain in peak form, but also because of the life-altering decision to come into a gaming house, leaving behind friends and family for a completely new set of peers, expectations and responsibilities. Of course, with experience these transitions become less traumatic; but for the very young, the dramatic shift in their environment and support can lead to difficulty fitting into the team's ideal dynamic.

'It's true that by going quickly from nowhere to the spotlight of eSports can alter a player's attitude and behaviour,' says Sättermon. 'But to avoid operating the onboarding and management of a new player or team on a "hit or miss" basis, we do spend quite some time interviewing them, and learning more about him or her. Aside from our early procedures, we do eventually place the new talent – or sometimes talents – in a professional environment that is run by a full-time team of managers and in most cases also coaches.

'We constantly train our staff to ensure that we provide an atmosphere where the team's parts, its individual players, work towards the same direction and goals, and they are also able to quickly pay additional attention when things do go wrong. You can certainly never protect yourself from individuals that are going rogue, but by being mindful during recruitment and consistent with our team management it's very rare that we have issues with players falling off the grid.'

In July 2016, Fnatic did have to part with one of its players. Gamsu, who'd joined seven months earlier alongside Spirit, was let go by the team, making way for new top-laner Kikis. The official statement was brief, but clear:

It comes with a heavy heart that we must part ways with Gamsu. However, it has become clear to us that our organisational goals and ideals are not aligned. At Fnatic, our priority is performing at the highest level whilst simultaneously securing the best possible future for our organisation. Following an evaluation with the whole team, Fnatic and Gamsu have mutually decided to part ways. Our management team will work hard to support Gamsu, making sure he can continue his career as a professional gamer, wherever he decides to go.

Thank you Gamsu for everything you have done for the team! We wish you the best of luck in the future.

As of early August 2016, Gamsu is still without a team. Stewart wrote a little about the change in player personnel in late July, on the *League of Legends* Championship Series website, in an article headlined 'Life of an LCS Manager':

Removing Gamsu and bringing Kikis was a difficult decision, and due to the time frame we had to move quickly. It was up to me to coordinate with G2, Fnatic and Kikis, and many things need to be considered: not only the most important factors such as buyout price and player contract, but other essential aspects such as flights/travel for both players, web announcements coordination, Fnatic jerseys with Kikis on the back etc. I didn't get much sleep over the few days change took place, but in situations like this you have to make sacrifices to make sure everything is perfect.

Fnatic also made the decision, after a fifth-placed finish in the summer season of the LCS, to part ways with Deilor, at least in a coaching capacity. 'Today, it is with great sadness that we announce that Luis "Deilor" Sevilla is stepping down as our *League of Legends* head coach,' began a statement posted to the team's website on 6 August.

> [He propelled] the team to never seen before heights by guiding them through an undefeated 18–0 split . . . as well as reaching the Semi Finals at Worlds last year. Unfortunately, with highs often come lows and rebuilding our lineup . . . [has] proved to be more challenging than expected. Because of recent results [the summer split finish] . . . Luis and the . . . management team mutually agreed that him stepping down is the correct course of action . . .
>
> We want to thank Deilor for all the passion, hard work and dedication he brought to Fnatic. We hope to be working with him again on other projects in the near future.

Playing to Your Strengths, and Handling the Pressure

With so much pressure on players to win, to reach the peak of their potential and stay there, at an age where a lot of peers would be starting to hang out in bars and generally enjoy the perks of being young, with expendable money and their whole life ahead of them, it's inevitable that cracks can appear.

'Results *always* matter,' says Yahoo eSports content creator Michael Martin, a specialist in the competitive fighting game scene, an area of eSports every bit as susceptible to player crisis as team-based disciplines like *League of Legends*. 'It matters to spectators, a player's peers, and potential sponsors. Winning puts a lot of pressure on players. People expect results. I've heard of sponsors that require players to finish in so many top eights, or finals, in fighting game tournaments, or they'll lose their sponsorship.

'The most distressing thing to me is a player who can't deal with the stress and pressure of competition,' he continues. 'Depression and anxiety aren't things we talk about enough, and I think it takes a collective effort to make sure the players are on stable ground. Players can burn out because they aren't used to the pressure, success and grind to stay relevant. In some cases, they burn out because they've hit their peak and there's nothing left for them to accomplish unless, maybe, a new game comes along.

'If a player is sponsored, or part of a big team, what is that organisation doing to help their players? Are they invested in helping players in times of need, or is the organisation just there to provide them a shirt to wear when the player appears on a live stream? On top of that, there's pressure being sponsored. Now you represent yourself *and* your sponsor as a brand. Is the organisation helping them learn how to do that? This is all new territory for a lot of people, both players and organisations, as eSports grows.'

As head coach, Deilor would often be in the firing line of fans' ire, should results not go the team's way. 'People on Twitter constantly tell me how to do my job,' he says. 'I'd get emails, too, telling me how bad I am for the team. But this is normal. It's important for me, and the players, that this doesn't get to us. This type of sport, unlike traditional sports, is a lot closer connected to the fans.

'With regular sports, a player might tweet something, and it's like it's behind glass. That's how that communication feels. Whatever they might say, you can't touch them; it's like they're in a showroom, in a store, and you can't afford them. But someone like Rekkles, he has a massive fan base, and you can go to the LCS and shake his hand, get an autograph, and talk to him for a couple of minutes. It's so much closer. And these guys are on Facebook constantly, tweeting daily. All the professionals read Reddit. So it's important that you don't feel destroyed by the media, or the fans, when you've had a bad game. All of these guys have really thick skins.

'As a new player, if you believe what other people are saying about you too much, that's going to disturb your performance. You're going to start doing things, in the games, to look good, or because someone else suggested it, rather than to win. It's really important to understand that other people, outside of your team, while of course they have their opinions, they're not important to your game plans. You can love and appreciate the fans, and listen to them; but make sure that you respect the line between personality and professionalism.'

This is something that Rekkles himself respects, and he appreciates how being in an organisation like Fnatic is beneficial to him overcoming the pressures of the game, and this way of life. 'I would say that I feel a different pressure nowadays, compared to when I started,' he says. 'But I don't think that's because of becoming famous. I think it's the difference between playing tournaments for fun, while I was going to school, while the whole thing was new to me; compared to now, living in Berlin, playing *League of Legends* as a full-time job, and putting everything on the table for it to succeed. That's why the pressure becomes so immense at times. But I wouldn't say that the pressure of the people that believe in me is overtaking me. I think they understand that you can't win every game, and be the best at all times. I've always been kind of lucky with that front. People have always had my back, through thick and thin.'

As the senior player in Fnatic's *League* team, YellOwStaR is well positioned to explain how a professional maintains their competitive level, when all other stresses are put to the side and it's all about focusing on your game, and how to take it even further.

'It's always about playing against the very best out there,' he says. 'You never want to practise against a mediocre team, in scrims or wherever, as that can make you worse. At the same time, if you're practising against someone who is good enough to do so, they'll begin to copy you. So when you're at the top, it's hard to stay there, because you have to always be innovative, creative, and come up with a lot of new ideas. But whoever you practise against, they will learn a lot from you and if they're good enough, and pay close enough attention, they will catch up to you eventually. So it's really tough – you don't want to give away your secrets.

'Even at the very top level, you do see other teams play how you have in the past. I was talking to Mithy from Origen [Alfonso Rodriguez, now playing support for G2], not so long ago. He told me that they weren't playing to their best to begin with in 2015, but since we were doing well, and they were practising with us, they actually learned a lot from Fnatic. They didn't have the same drive to win, maybe, but Fnatic's form in dragging Europe up made them want to follow. So they were playing to keep up with us. That's what he told me. They learned so much from us that they were nearly at the same level as our team. That's probably why it was so close when we played them at the Worlds that year.'

The making of a pro-player isn't just about the mechanical side of the game, then, but also the strength to resist, or at least respect, the impossible expectation of fans, the decency to toe the line when it comes to discipline both online and off it, and constantly playing against the best out there. As *League of Legends*, and eSports in general, grows and grows, there will be inevitable casualties – but with fast fingers and a level head, the brightest stars of the LCS and beyond will only continue to shine.

8

The Captain's Story: YellOwStaR in His Own Words

In Fnatic, when we're playing and practising, I do all I can to encourage the team. I notice a lot of details, sometimes things that other players miss, perhaps because of my experience – I've had six years of playing at this pace, since I began competing in *League of Legends* in 2010. I've always been the guy who wants to put things together in his head, to make things work, and that extends beyond the game. I can see when someone in the team is down, is sad, and I'll speak to them about what's going on. I don't want our players not to be happy.

I know, though, that even when that guy says yes, he's fine, that he might not be, because that's what young men do. And you know when that is happening to a player, in the middle of a game. You know it because you live with these people. I'm around them all day for seven days a week. You notice the smallest things.

As a human being, I've always looked out for others, and having a work environment with a positive atmosphere is going to make everything easier, and more comfortable, especially when you live with these people too. And I think that's something other teams neglect to consider. They might go out and get the best players, and they think that means they'll automatically be the best team. But it really doesn't work like that. It's just not true. A team formed of superstars will always have people playing for themselves, not for each other.

Formative Play

My relationship with video games began early. I have an older brother, and I started playing games with him when I was just two years old. He is two and a half years older than me, but even back then he really wanted to teach me how to play too, I think mainly because he didn't enjoy playing the games on his own. We played console games – we had a Nintendo 64 (N64), at home in France, and a Mega Drive, too. I can remember not being able to hold the controllers properly, but nevertheless, my brother stuck at it, and he taught me how to play a lot of games. Of course, back then, and for years after, we were just playing for fun – I had no idea about competitive gaming, or if I wanted to become the best at a particular game, or anything like that.

My cousins would come over to play video games with us, too, or we'd go to their house, and we'd play all evening long. They're some ten years older than me, but while I was the youngest in the group, I never wanted just to sit there and watch. And also, I didn't want them to include me in their games only to be nice, or out of a sense of pity. I was always thinking: I want them to accept me because I'm good enough, and not for any other reason. So, I think I must have been about eight years old when I decided I wanted to get good at the games I was playing. I started to be able to compete with them, and they really enjoyed playing with me, and it was at that age that I got into *StarCraft* too, as we'd got a PC in the home by then.

On the N64, I'd play *Mario Party* with my brother and cousins, and then *GoldenEye 007* and *Mario Kart* when I was a bit older. We would play the four-player split-screen mode on *GoldenEye*. But actually, I was only playing a first-person shooter because I was following what other people were playing – I wanted to play whatever my brother was playing. And it was my brother who got me into *StarCraft*. I would watch him play it, all the time, and I just had to try it. As it turned out, I got into it quite easily.

I wouldn't say that I became addicted to *StarCraft*, but it was the only game I put many, many hours of play into back then. I was having a lot of fun playing it, but there was something else to the game too, that the Nintendo games didn't give me. I was able to compare myself with other players, around the world, using the online rankings. Looking back, I think that's where my competitive side started.

My brother has always helped me get into certain games – after *StarCraft*, when I was maybe thirteen, he began playing *Warcraft III*, and so I did, too. I was reluctant to play it at first – honestly, I thought it looked terrible. But everyone was switching to it, all of my friends. I thought that if I just went ahead and made the switch, I'd be really bad at it, having put so much time into *StarCraft*; so I waited to make my move, and asked my brother all sorts of questions about it. He gave me a lot of advice, and that knowledge helped me get ahead in the game, at an early stage. I played that game until I was eighteen, when I switched to *League of Legends*. I'm not someone who can play a variety of video games – I've always mostly chosen one, and stuck at it, and done whatever I can to be very good at it. Some of the guys at Fnatic play other games on their day off, like *Overwatch*, or the latest *Call of Duty*. But I only stick to the one game, to *this* game. Honestly, I don't find it fun to play anything else.

And I do still enjoy the game – it's a *fun* game. In my opinion, if you want to be able to perform in *League of Legends*, you *have* to be able to enjoy it. If you don't really like it, and you see playing the game as a pain, like it's just a job to you, it's your work and nothing else, then it's not something that's going to be any fun. I don't see this as a chore, but I've seen this behaviour in other play-ers – some are actually very vocal about it, and say, 'This is my job, even though I don't enjoy playing the game any more, and I just have to do it.' And they say it publicly. For me that's a shame, because they're admitting it on social media. It really affects a player's image. But it's their choice, I suppose.

Parental Guidance

My parents were not initially supportive of my ambi-tion to become a professional gamer, but they've had a very hard life, and something like this, as a career, was very hard for them to understand at first. They were both born in Cambodia, and they had to fight to escape the genocides that swept the country in the 1970s. They managed it after three years of trying, leaving the war at home behind them to start a new life in France. But they arrived with nothing, didn't know the language and had hardly any support. It was extremely difficult for them, building a new life from the ground up in a strange country.

So for them, it was hard to accept that we – my brother and I – could spend quite so long as we did playing video games. They didn't consider that productive, at the beginning. But they told us: 'If you guys are responsible enough with school, and you're getting good grades, good marks, and everything is working well, then okay, during your free time you can play video games.' But they still wanted us to diversify our activities, so we were encouraged to read, to play outside, to do sports. And we thought that was a good deal. We had to respect that our parents were working a lot, working very hard, to support us. We wanted to be good kids, and not make trouble. So that deal worked: we'd be good students, so that we could play video games.

I was a better gamer than my brother, but he began to really support me. I still had no idea what eSports was, though, until I was playing *Warcraft III* one time, and someone online told me about them. I was playing at a good level, and they said to me, 'Why don't you take part in this online tournament?' Did such a thing exist? Of course it did, sure, so I just had to give it a try. I could simply compete from home, so no travel meant that my parents didn't suspect anything – to them, I was only doing what I normally did on a Saturday, sitting down playing games. But I performed really well, and other people in the *Warcraft III* community, in France, noticed me. And then the offer came in.

I was still only fifteen, so when a manager from a team offered me the chance to play in an offline tournament, I knew I needed to talk about it with my parents. They'd have to agree to my attending. But they had no idea about the scene, about what to expect – and they were much too busy to take me. The tournament was on a weekend, and I promised them I'd do my homework, and that I'd be all right. I was playing people much older than I was, people who were twenty years old. And I came third, out of the whole of France, just out of nowhere. That got people asking who I was. I was invited to join a team, and then my dad had to acknowledge that this was a big deal. He'd been aware of it before, but at that time there was no real salary to speak of. To him, I'd just been playing at home, playing normally, on the weekends so as not to interrupt my other activities.

The only problem was that I was a minor, still under eighteen, when I was competing in *Warcraft III*, which I did for a French team, Millenium. So if I travelled I needed someone to chaperone me. I had a friend in the same team who was older than me, who was willing to be that person, basically to be my guardian. And that's where it started for me, as an amateur. I went on to win the ESWC (Electronic Sports World Convention) French Championship in 2009, when I played under the name of Psyko.

Changing the Game

When I switched to *League of Legends* in 2009 – again because of a tip-off from my brother, who thought I'd like it – I started to play more international tournaments. Before, with *Warcraft III*, I was really only playing in France, going around the country. With *League of Legends*, the first tournament I played was in Germany. I was still in college at the time, but my studies were not going well. That's where my brother and I differ – he's always been a good student, with no trouble in that department, but he's never truly been a good gamer. My parents were worried – they'd seen me playing video games a lot, and now I was failing at school, despite the deal we'd made to make college a priority.

I was somewhere between these two stools, and I had to make a choice on where to sit. Which did I actually want to do: school or gaming? For me it was clear: I was more interested in competing in video games than I was in going to college. So I failed that year in school; but in the same year, 2011, with the against All authority team, I qualified for the *League of Legends* World Championship, where we ended up taking second place behind Fnatic. My parents, though, were upset that I'd chosen to play video games, instead of concentrating on graduating.

In 2011, my parents really had no idea how big eSports was, let alone how big it could become. It certainly wasn't as big then as it is today. They weren't proud of me, for what I'd achieved at the World Championship, because they didn't have the context – all they cared about was their children having a secure future for themselves, having careers, all of that. So they were very worried about my situation. I told them I'd only messed up one year of school, and that was all right; and the next year I worked hard on my studies, even while taking part in tournaments. Sometimes I'd miss a whole week of classes, but I had friends who'd take notes for me so I could catch up. My parents began to trust me – they saw that I was working hard. And I passed that year, even while competing in *League of Legends* for Millenium – I moved teams after the first World Championships, along with a lot of the against All authority *League* players.

Then, in 2013, after I'd played for a few teams, I was offered a contract from Fnatic. My parents realised this was a serious offer. I convinced them that it was too good an opportunity to miss, and that I should take it. My brother and cousins agreed, and they all supported me. This was a once-in-a-lifetime opportunity – I had to go for it. If it meant missing a year of college, that's nothing in life. I could make the time up if playing did not work out. The contract said that I would be taken care of, that I'd have a place to stay, to live, even though it's abroad. I'd have a house and everything would be covered, and when my parents saw that they told me, 'Okay, you can do it for a year, and let's see how you perform, and how happy you are.'

They soon saw that it was making me happy, and that I was growing up a lot – moving to Berlin to live in the team's gaming house made me more independent, and more confident too. I used to be incredibly shy. But in this business you meet a lot of people, and you have to talk a lot. You work with many others, and you're always learning so much about marketing and communication. So eSports has given me many skills, beyond just being able to click a mouse incredibly well.

My cousins, who live in America, would watch me play on streams. They told my uncle, my dad's brother, that they'd been watching me. Later, when speaking on the phone, my uncle explained to my dad that I was sort of famous these days. My dad brought that up with me and I just said, 'Well, I don't know about that. I'm just doing my thing, you know.' That's how all this started between Fnatic and myself.

In Position

When I started playing *League of Legends*, I wasn't playing in the support role, like I do nowadays – I was playing AD carry. I was the marksman, dishing out the damage, cleaning up, and I had a lot of fun in that role. But I've always been someone who wants to be in control of what he did, and also sort of how the team plays overall. So, over the years, I've been developing a greater knowledge of the game, and how we should work together as a team to win games. I was trying to make calls during the game, but I saw that it was affecting my AD carry performances, because I couldn't focus on so many things at the same time to make it work. I was getting caught in positions that could lose us games – I couldn't keep playing so riskily.

In Fnatic, Rekkles was playing AD carry as well, but he was too young to compete back in 2013, because of the age restriction. He was one year too young – sixteen, when you have to be seventeen to play in the LCS. So I was AD carry – but we knew when he turned seventeen, he'd step in. And when that time came, I had to make a choice: did I really want to play support? It was a risky move for the team, because I had no prior experience in the role. But my teammates trusted me. If it hadn't worked out, it would have dragged the whole team down, and we would not have qualified for the World Championships in 2015. And that wouldn't have affected only the team negatively, but the Fnatic brand as well, so I was very aware of how much I had to do, not to disappoint everyone.

In 2015, when I switched, I felt comfortable in the support role after just two months – which is actually a long time, considering all the stuff we had to go through. We performed well in the end, of course, reaching the semi-final in 2015, and that's when people realised Fnatic's *League of Legends* team was a force again. I was so proud. The support role was fitting me very well.

It was a fantastic change from Fnatic's year before that. In 2014, I was upset that our team didn't get to go further in the World Championships – we went out in the group stage. I was questioning myself a lot, and wondering what had gone wrong. We'd practised so much, and yet we were not able to perform. So what was the point in keeping going? I was doubting myself; I had a lot of internal worries. We were practising for more than fifteen hours a day – what more could we do?

I understood, though, that of course it's a team game, and if everyone is not working towards the same goal, that's a problem. I realised I shouldn't be too harsh on myself, but I kept asking: why did we fail? What can I do better, to improve personally, and for the team? I decided then not to give up – and at that point my dad was very supportive. He snapped me out of thinking that our failure was all my fault, and he told me to keep going. Everyone was supporting me. And I had a feeling that I owed Fnatic – if I wasn't playing for them, basically they'd have no *League of Legends* team, because the team split apart in 2014. Rekkles left for Alliance, and xPeke to form Origen. I was so grateful and loyal to Fnatic, though, because of the opportunity they'd given me to be a pro-gamer, that I had to give something back.

The American Dream

So I stayed, and I built a new team – that's when Febiven came in, with Reignover, Steelback and Huni, before

Rekkles returned in the spring of 2015 – and then we surprised everyone by overperforming at the next World Championships. Nobody expected us to play as well as we did. We won Spring Split with four completely new members, with no experience of playing on stage; and then during Summer Split we did a perfect Split, which was a new record. After the Worlds, though, the team broke apart again, and I wondered if maybe the time was right for me to leave, too.

I was offered the opportunity to play somewhere else, and one of the offers I received was from the United States, with one of the biggest organisations, Team SoloMid, based in Santa Monica. I thought that working in another organisation, with new people, in a new environment, would be a good thing. I always want to experience more, all that I can, and after spending three years in the same place, in the same country, I felt as though it was the right time for a change. Even now, I don't know where I will ultimately end up living, where I will most enjoy myself. I always want to see more of the world. So I took that opportunity in late 2015, but it turned out to be not so great.

Playing with TSM taught me plenty, and it was helpful in several ways. I had to deal with new situations, new people. I had to learn a lot about myself, about how to work with these strangers and their different systems. I had to work on new ways to solve issues. There were some amazing people there, but overall, I was not happy living in the US. Nevertheless, I'm grateful that I managed to learn so much from the experience. I needed to be somewhere I could live and grow happily, though, for the sake of my career, and that's why I decided to come back: Fnatic and Berlin. They both feel like home. But when you hear about the West Coast, the American Dream, of course you're going to give it a shot. I was living in Los Angeles. I had family there, and I'd spent holidays there, so I was like: Hell, yeah. But I genuinely prefer to be in Europe – and when I'm happier, I perform better.

When I was at TSM, all the relationships in my daily life were great. I got along with everyone there, when we weren't playing. But when it came down to work, ethics and compromises, it was so difficult to change them, to my way of thinking, at all. I was always willing to adapt, but they were not going to give that back. It was very frustrating. If something wasn't working, they would point their fingers at me, as if I was the bad guy. Or at least that was the feeling I was getting. I even asked the manager if he'd bench me – and offered to bench myself if he wouldn't. But he told me the team had no better option than to keep me where I was, so I had to keep playing. I often thought about stepping down before I finally left at the end of the North America season, to come back to Fnatic.

That Winning Feeling

I try to enjoy all the moments I'm having in eSports, because I know this career can be incredibly short. The only times I can remember being genuinely sad were in 2014, when we were so disappointed at not performing to our standards. Honestly, I was crushed, and I thought about leaving eSports altogether. What kept me going was the support I had from my family, and from Fnatic. They reassured me that it wasn't my fault; but I'm always thinking, even when we're winning, about what I can do better and how I can improve. You can *always* do better, if you want to.

The proudest moment I've had wasn't the winning of a tournament, but probably when I successfully switched from AD carry to support. We could have gone for other options – the team could have looked for a more natural support player. But I made the move, and, honestly, I exceeded even my own expectations, which hadn't seemed likely at the beginning because I was quite shaky. But then we got results, and we began to show our quality on stage. That was a great feeling. We finally got recognition. Our

Above: The first Fnatic kill of the 2016 Summer Split.

Below: Rekkles triple kill against G2 during the 2016 Summer Split.

perfect score at Summer Split 2015 is obviously a great achievement, but for me, oddly, it's nothing special. It was a consequence of all our hard work.

When you go out on to the stage, the only thing you're thinking about is performing. So when you're focused, you don't see anything else but what's on the screen at that time. You barely hear the crowd, and most of the time you don't notice them. And even when you win, you're still so intensely focused on the game that it's all you're able to think about. You still enjoy the moment – but you're always focusing on what game is coming up next. For me, I have a weird mindset where I am always looking to the future, rather than focusing on the moment that's happening right then. I've always cared about what's next; I can never rest. If the team is winning, you have no holiday, basically. You have to live for work, to be able to do this.

YellOwStaR's Career in League

Team history

September 2010–June 2011 and November 2011–May 2012: against All authority

June–October 2011 and June–July 2012: Millenium

July–December 2012: SK Gaming

January 2013–December 2015 and May 2016–present:
  Fnatic

December 2015–May 2016: Team SoloMid

Key achievements

June 2011: Runner-up, season one World Championship
  with against All authority

April 2013: winner, EU LCS Spring Playoffs with Fnatic

August 2013: winner, EU LCS Summer Playoffs with
  Fnatic

September 2013: semi-finalist, season three World
  Championship with Fnatic

April 2014: winner, EU LCS Spring Playoffs with Fnatic

April 2015: winner, EU LCS Spring Playoffs with Fnatic

August 2015: winner, EU LCS Summer Playoffs with
  Fnatic

October 2015: semi-finalist, season five World
  Championship with Fnatic

April 2016: runner-up, NA LCS Spring Playoffs with
  Team SoloMid

9

The God Slayer Speaks:
Febiven in His Own Words

There is no luck in professional gaming, in *League of Legends*. We don't believe in it at Fnatic. And you can't have a bad day, either. When you lose against a team you know is not as good as yours, that isn't down to luck – it's because you played worse than they did on the day.

You have to avoid falling into too much negativity when that happens, and look at what you did wrong as a team that led to that defeat. We use the defeats to work out how we can improve, as it's only when you lose that the problems you have as a team are really highlighted clearly. When you're winning everything, like we have done, and you practise the same ways, then other teams can catch up with you and counter the way in which you're playing. That puts you a week behind. But when another team beats you, you see their hand, and you hope they become overconfident so that you can do the same to them and take advantage of, I suppose, their complacency. When you're winning, you can be reluctant to change how you're winning, but that will enable the other teams to work out how you're doing it, and turn it against you.

If we're facing a good team, instead of a lower-tier team, I think it's harder to prepare – but it's also easier, because we get a lot of motivation from playing against the best. When I'm playing against a really good mid-laner, I'm on my 'A' level.

Game Boy

I started playing console games at home in the Netherlands, on a Nintendo GameCube. I was on *Mario Kart* a lot. Before that, I'd play on a Game Boy. That was the first thing I picked up. We had a PlayStation at home, too, but then we got a computer, a PC, and I got into playing on that, too. I come from a big family – I'm one of six siblings – so there were always people playing video games in the house. In particular, my two brothers and I would play against each other. Eventually I stuck with the

PC as I found the games I was playing on it more fun. And I played a lot.

When it came to online games, I first started playing *RuneScape*, just with my friends. That was for five years (or something like that). I'd occasionally drop into *World of Warcraft*, but one day I realised that I found it kind of boring, and a friend suggested I take a look at *League of Legends*. So I downloaded it, played for a bit – and I *kept* playing it.

I didn't like *League of Legends* straight away. It took months to get into it. I am still learning, too, still adapting. There is no player who is perfect every game, and even if you have what you *think* is a perfect game, there will always be something you could have done better. Like, how fast are you clicking? What is your reaction speed? You can always build those up, but while also being realistic with yourself. If you keep getting hit, you mustn't think there's nothing you can do – you have to believe that you can learn to dodge faster. There are always things to improve on: your accuracy, how many times you're getting hit by skill shots, how you are acting outside of the game. It's a constant learning process, both inside and out of the game.

Playing a new game is always more fun than what you've been playing before, of course, and I honestly did find *League of Legends* a lot of fun to play, as I was learning how to. I was just jumping around with a champion, not really knowing what I was doing. Then I began to watch some tournaments, and that gave me the motivation to play more, and to get better. To begin with, though, I was only playing for fun. I wasn't paying much attention at first to the professional competitive scene, though I'd seen the World Championships before I became serious myself, around season two.

Playing on the ladder, before coming into a team, was very rewarding. The higher I got on it, the greater my motivation was to get even higher. I stopped playing normal games every day, against my friends, because it felt like a waste of time. I'd just beat them, over and over, for no real reward. So I started playing a lot more alone, in Challenger.

I earned a reputation as one of the best with the champion Riven, though I obviously wasn't only playing as her – but whenever she was available, I would choose her. Why not? It was like putting on a comfy pair of shoes. I think if you want to achieve a high level, early, play as the same champion all the time. And the higher you get, the easier it is to see how other people play as other champions. I just never saw the point of playing as other champions – it takes more time, you get more frustrated, and you win less often. I mastered Riven, and then I reached the point where I started seeing her banned, so I had to play as other champions. You *have* to get good across a range of champions, really, to be at a level where going professional is an option.

When you're exclusively playing *League of Legends*, you have to know your way around a handful of champions. It's not as if I was even trying to get good, when I was coming up with Riven, because I don't think at the time I knew how to. I was just playing to win, and being tough. I'd get frustrated with it, but I'd press on, to get higher in the rankings. But I had to learn how to play with new champions to maintain my position.

I climbed to the top ten in Challenger with four accounts, and I was the only player in that situation. I was contacted by other Challenger players, and we made a team together. We were called Apples is sour, and we reached the top position on the European ranked five-versus-five Challenger series. That led to Cloud9 contacting us, because they wanted a Challenger team, and we were basically the best in Europe. So we became their European Challenger team in early 2014, Cloud9 Eclipse.

The Path to Fnatic

We won a lot with Cloud9, pretty much everything we could. We had to change organisation though, later in 2014, because a ruling came in that you could not operate two teams in different territories, and Cloud9 is an American team. So its European team disbanded, and I went to H2k; I played a lot of tournaments with them for a year. I would travel to London occasionally, because that's where H2k is based, and played many tournaments at home in the Netherlands. Back then I was still going to school, and still playing football, on top of *League*.

I tasted success with H2k. We placed first at the 2014 European Challenger Series Summer Playoffs, and had taken top spot in the Summer Series of that June, where we beat Ninjas in Pyjamas, a great team at the time that would always push us. But I wasn't all that happy there – well, not as happy as I am now. There was a lot of stuff going on, and I couldn't get along with certain teammates. I just couldn't gel there. So I decided to leave, and was a free agent at the end of 2014, going into 2015 looking for a team.

That's when I learned about Fnatic's interest. Now, when the best organisation in Europe comes and asks you to join them, and you *decline* it, you're a bit stupid. So I went for it, because I knew it'd give me a high chance of being successful. The team was going through a lot of changes, but I was ready for a new experience. I knew Fnatic was well structured, and that it had a massive fan base, and these factors helped me make my decision pretty easily.

The team wasn't in the best shape, though. In December 2014, Fnatic was falling apart. Four players left its *League of Legends* team. At the time, I was the best free agent possible for Fnatic, so they asked me and I came into the house in January 2015; this has been me ever since.

As an organisation, Fnatic's goal is always to be number one. But if we're ever *not* number one, we're trying to get there. We're always trying to get to that point and stay there. That's a massively motivating thing for me.

Growing Up on a World Stage

I came into Fnatic's Berlin house when I'd just turned eighteen. It was my first time living away from home, and it still is. It was a hard period of adjustment for me because, honestly, back home, I was always pretty spoiled. My parents got me everything I wanted, and I could play video games there all the time. They'd ask me why I was spending so long in front of the computer, and I'd tell them to wait, and that I'd show them what I was working towards. I'd tell them this every night over dinner, around the table: that I had my sights set on becoming a professional gamer.

When I first left home it was very hard for me – and it was hard for my mum, and my dad, too. I'd never left before, certainly not for a long time – only for those trips to London, really, and some tournaments. I wasn't scared about not performing well, once I was in Berlin, but when I got here it was definitely a bit of a culture shock. All of a sudden I was expected to act and behave in certain ways that I was not used to. It took me a little time to adjust to how to handle these things, and at first I was in a bad way.

I was good at playing the game, but at eighteen, my brain was still that of a little kid, maybe because my life had been quite sheltered up until then. So when I came here, people were on at me to do things like – and this sounds silly – cut my nails, and I'd think: Why the fuck do I care about cutting my nails? So, small things like that, being told to do things, could actually get me quite frustrated. Why would anyone else care that my nails were not cut? And cleaning, washing my clothes, I'd never done that at my own home. I didn't have my mum any more and, honestly, that was a definite period of adjustment.

When I was a rookie, in the Splits in 2015, I had very low confidence. I was young, and still growing up, and I also thought I was worse than the other players here – which I actually *was*. It put a lot of pressure on me to perform, and I didn't want to let my team down; I didn't want to get carried by the others, either. So I had a hard time gaining confidence.

Sometimes I'd be incredibly nervous before games, depending on who I'd be playing. If I was playing a good mid-laner, I'd be especially nervous; but I'd be nervous before every game, really. That's always normal, but sometimes it'd be a bit extreme.

In Position

The game itself changes a lot, so my way into playing mid-lane was down to the number of champions I liked in that position. These were champions who were fast. You're in the centre of the map, so you can help everywhere else, and bring resources fairly quickly to you if you need them. You definitely need to be quite a demanding person to play in the mid-lane, because you're always asking your team to play around you.

Every time the game is patched, though, you have to adjust your role, and that affects the entire team. You're always looking for the best plays at the time, on the fly, so when you're the mid-laner you have to be incredibly flexible.

How the game in question is going will have a big influence on where the mid-laner is going, and how they're acting. If you're needed to help your teammates elsewhere on the map, you're going to have to go and do that. But if your own mid-lane game is going very strongly, they will come and centre themselves around you.

In terms of champions right now, I like Azir, Viktor and LeBlanc. Those are my favourites for this season. I'd say, though, that they're champions best suited to people with experience, as there are some hard mechanics in there, amongst their abilities. You *can* play every champion as a beginner, but you won't be a good mid-laner if you're missing half your creeps every game. What makes you a good mid-laner is simply being good across every aspect. Stay flexible, play a lot of champions, never miss a creep, maintain good communication, don't let yourself tilt.

Stress Management and God Slaying

Being in this house, sometimes things can become stressful, and when they do I go to the gym, or I go chill with friends. It's important to find some space, to give yourself some space to not play *League* all the time. If you *only* play *League*, and you don't think about what is wrong with your teammate relationships, it's going to stack up and explode one day, and you won't know what is going on.

When there is a problem, of course, we try to talk about it. But then there are also things that don't get talked about for fear of them causing further tension. But not discussing them can be worse. I think some important stuff gets talked about, while other things we just sort of forget about. I guess it can be hard for young men to show their emotions when they're around each other.

While it's healthy to take breaks from the game, I actually play as much as possible. Even when my parents are visiting, I'm still spending a lot of time on *League*. Of course, I'm always happy when people come to visit me in Berlin; but when we're on a bad run, it gives you the feeling that you have to turn it around, and it's hard to focus on anything else but fixing that form. I never really think I need a 'free' day, unless I'm feeling stressed out, and that is only ever very rarely the case.

Nowadays, I think I consider myself famous in the eSports world – and that's mainly because I'm at Fnatic, the biggest organisation. But also because I killed Faker, twice, at the 2015 Mid-Season Invitational in Florida. We didn't win that tournament – we finished in the third and fourth spots, losing to SK in the semi-final – but I took Faker out twice in those games. That was the first time anyone had ever done that to him – he's maybe the best mid-laner in the world. People called him the god of his position, so I'm the God Slayer.

Because of that, I think I have a lot of Chinese and South Korean fans – when Huni and Reignover were at Fnatic, they told me that if I went to South Korea, every girl would like me. So I suppose I'm famous everywhere in the world. And I like being recognised. On the street, or on social media. It means that I mean something to fans, and that's pretty cool.

Trusting in Your Teammates

There are two ways of acting, basically, when you're in the middle of a game. You either back off when your teammates tell you to, listening to their calls, or you ignore them and go for the play you think is correct. Then, if it fails, of course that will cause frustration among your teammates. But when you're so sure it's the right play, you *have* to go for it. After the game, you tell whoever told you to hold back that you had the right play. It's all about doing the right thing, and getting the result.

But games can be won and lost in the draft phase, when we're picking our champions. We look closely at what champions the other teams are using, and prepare scenarios for the drafting phase. We look over other teams' previous games to see how they play, to build our own counter-plays. No team is perfect, and every one will make mistakes, so there will always be weaknesses to exploit.

Usually if you 'lose' in the draft phase, and the opposition has totally outpicked you, you'll feel that the game's over before it has even started. But when you've got what appear to be the weaker champions, you can always win if the other team plays incorrectly. It really all depends on how well the opponent plays with those better champions. They *should* win every time, but that's not always the case.

Within your own team, you aim to pick champions who fit together, who complement each other. You pick, too, to be good against your enemies, in each position. Usually the draft can be even, as there are just so many champions to pick from, but in every patch some will become very overpowered. That's another reason why you can't just play the same few champions – there's a strong chance that one patch or another will alter the way they match up to others.

You can get a read on which character to try yourself by looking at the win rates for certain champions, across the regions. If someone has a good win rate with one in particular, then obviously you're going to try it yourself, because that means *something* is going on with them. You should really try every champion, and take yourself out of your comfort zone, otherwise you're never going to learn the deeper game.

That said, there are a lot of champions who are *never* played, because they're pretty useless, so Riot could just lose them. That, or they should make them better. I suppose people play casually with all the champions, so maybe that's why they stick around; but maybe only half of them get a look in competitively.

At Fnatic, we always play as a team, and listen to each other as we play. But in practice, and scrims, we'll have to deal with 'animals', sometimes. That's what we call each other, animals, when we're playing over-aggressively. And when someone is, they usually need to be reined in a bit.

Career Highs and Future Hopes

I can't say that I've experienced a real low in my career so far. Losing in the semi-finals at the Worlds in 2015, in Brussels, was tough to take, of course – but getting that far was still a great achievement, and I don't feel so bad about it in hindsight. I think I'm always on something of a high playing with this team.

A very personal highlight of my time with Fnatic, though, was when we played in Rotterdam, at the 2016

Spring Playoffs. We came third, and winning that match, in front of 10,000 people shouting my name, and my whole family, it felt as though we'd won the final. It was special, too, as the team we beat to finish third was H2k. I was on stage afterwards, holding a Dutch flag. It was quite emotional. But while so many friends and family were there, I don't much think about them while playing – just before and after the game, never during. I'm rarely distracted from the game at all, unless the crowd is really screaming. I suppose a streaker running on to the stage might turn my eye, but that hasn't happened yet.

I see *League* as a young man's game – a lot of the best players out there are aged between eighteen and twenty. It might be because your responsiveness slows down as you get older, although I don't think that's a massive factor. People leaving the game has more to do with their own motivation. To be honest, I wonder myself about what I'll be doing five years from now. I can see myself playing, and enjoying, this game for years to come, probably until I'm thirty, but beyond that? I'm not so sure. There's no way I'll be playing this game when I'm forty, assuming it's still around. I'll just play it for as long as I'm getting the most out of it – and until I think there's something cooler to do.

Febiven's Career in *League*

Team history

January–May 2014: Cloud9 Eclipse

May 2014–January 2015: H2k-Gaming

January 2015–present: Fnatic

Key achievements

February 2014: winner, EU Challenger Spring Series with Cloud9 Eclipse

March 2014: winner, Black Monster Cup Spring Europe with Cloud9 Eclipse

August 2014: winner, EU Challenger Series Summer Playoffs with H2k-Gaming

August 2015: winner, EU LCS Summer Playoffs with Fnatic

October 2015: semi-finalist, season five World Championship with Fnatic

April 2016: third place, EU LCS Spring Playoffs with Fnatic

10

Welcome, the Jungler: Spirit in His Own Words

I'm the jungler in the team, and that means I'm always looking to win the game – for the team, of course – and I *can* do that by taking on an enemy laner, by solo carrying proceedings. I have a lot of confidence – I always think I'm going to be able to change the way a game is going, to turn it to our advantage. But I'm always there to help my teammates – if they need assistance, I should go to them.

But the way I play, the position I fill, it's a hard thing to explain. In this role, you're moving all the time. I should always be making my teammates safe, and I'm communicating with them when enemies spawn. Both the jungler, and whoever is playing support, shouldn't *really* be focusing on kills; so I should be controlling the map, and understanding the whole game. I need to be seeing all of the map, and anticipating what the enemy is going to do in their lanes. It's a hard role to play.

Starting Young

I think my parents playing video games at home, when I lived in South Korea, is probably what got me so interested in them. I'd see my mum playing and say to her, 'I wanna try, too,' and the same with my dad. And I did get to play; I found it so much fun. My parents could see that I had some talent. So they were quite encouraging of me, in terms of enjoying video games.

When I was young, like around five or six years old, I started playing *StarCraft*. I think that's quite young to be playing a game like that. But it was where it started for me, my love of gaming, and of computers too, as basically I learned how to use them through playing the game. After school, I'd always be playing video games – and then when I got to about eight years old, I started playing *World of Warcraft*. I played a lot of different games, actually, because my parents would bring a lot of them into the house. So even if I'd not got into *StarCraft*, I had so many chances to get into games.

But when I told my parents I wanted to do this professionally, they weren't so sure. They got a little angry with me, actually. I remember them telling me not to do this. They didn't see it as something that would be good for my life, due to the long-term prospects, which didn't seem so positive at the time.

I'd felt the desire to become a professional gamer at a very young age. When I was thirteen, I wanted to be a pro *StarCraft* player. I told my mother, and she was really angry. To her, being a pro-gamer meant *just* playing games and nothing else, and it had a low salary, so it wasn't a very good job. She was against the idea, but I was adamant that I wanted to be a pro-gamer; I genuinely believed that I could be. So I didn't talk to my mum about it any more. I trained a lot, and I played tournaments both online and off, but I never told my mum about them, about what I was doing. I'd say things like, 'Mum, I'm just off to study for something,' or that I was going to see friends, but I'd be playing video games.

However, I was able to maintain my studies. My grades at school were actually very good, so my mum didn't ever think that I wasn't studying. My parents had no cause to worry about me in terms of how I was doing at school.

I accumulated 2,400 points playing solo queue, before I transitioned to being a pro-gamer. Back then, I used to play as a mid-laner, because I understood the champion mechanics for that position. I was in that role when I was playing in South Korea, playing solo queue. But I adjusted to jungler when I got into the pro-gamer world. I started as a mid-laner because I didn't understand the game all that well. I was playing only for me, not as part of a team, and I'd always try to win games myself. Later, I realised I had to learn the map better to succeed, and being the jungler was a good way to do that. And, actually, the role is a lot of fun. When I'm playing smart, the enemy jungler simply can't do anything. I can be quite mechanical in the role, or play with cunning, and I've been doing this since my second season.

South Korean Beginnings and Chinese Disappointment

I joined a *League of Legends* team, MVP Blue, in the summer of 2013, in the game's third season. This was when I was still at home – it was a South Korean team, and an offshoot, really, of a *StarCraft* team of the same name. Back then, they were maybe the worst team in the South Korean league, the LCK. But I had confidence that I could make the team better. And when we'd practise, we'd win every game. We did very well. In the first season, we met SK Telecom T1 (SKT), and they were an almost perfect team. Sadly we did lose to them, and missed out on going to the Worlds.

MVP Blue became Samsung Galaxy Blue just a few months after I joined, and I stayed there until October 2014. We were a good team – we won the HOT6iX Championship, an OGN (OnGameNet) tournament, in spring 2014, at which I had the best kills–deaths–assists ratio of any jungler.

I can remember a key moment while at Samsung, back in 2014. We were losing games, so many games. So one night we grouped together. We all started talking after dinner – and that went on until about 5 a.m. We just talked through every little thing, every point of how we were performing. It went on for, I think, six hours in total. And the next week, we near enough destroyed everyone. So that was a night with no sleep, of real in-depth analysis on how we were doing, and afterwards we won almost every game. That made it clear that we were all hungry to win. We all wanted to improve – and it took that time together to properly work out how we could as a team. The success followed – that felt truly special. We talked about things we'd never discussed before, and our relationship massively strengthened. Afterwards, we felt that we could turn any losing position around; that any little mistake in a league game didn't matter, we were still going to win. We played more like a team than ever before.

But I left Samsung in October 2014. I took a little break, and I think that's important for my career. If I want to be a pro-gamer for as long as I possibly can, then I think it's vital to have these pauses. It stops everything becoming overwhelming. At that point, *League of Legends* was starting to become popular in China, and teams there were beginning to offer some good salaries. So I decided to go there, to Team WE, who are actually the first eSports team in China.

The fan base in China was great, but the team didn't work out for me. In the South Korean league, the environment is well suited to being a pro-gamer. Everything is perfect, and you just focus on the game. When I played in China, the environment wasn't the same. At Team WE, if you were doing well, if you carried a game, you'd get a bonus on top of your salary. In South Korea, and in Europe, it's very much more a case of playing as a team. In China, I don't think there's such good synergy between teammates, because everyone is playing for themselves, without the level of communication we see in the European LCS. I would try to communicate with my teammates – I can speak Chinese, after all. But the Chinese culture itself seems to emphasise the doing of things alone. It's almost a bit selfish, so it's hard for players to build good relationships there with each other, and with the managers.

In South Korea, I'd always be talking to my teammates, suggesting different tactics. We'd try all manner of approaches, and discover between us what was the best way. That wasn't the case in China. There, you'd propose a way to play, someone else would disagree, just one person, and that was that, no discussion about it. No further conversation necessary: we wouldn't be pursuing that plan. And maybe I know why. At Team WE, we were all young, and when you're young, you're not good at taking criticism. People would get mad, and take everything personally. And I'd get mad, too, but I'd also think about how I could change what I was doing.

After each game in China, everyone would just watch the replay by themselves, and not share that experience or learn together. That's not healthy. If I see that something is wrong, but we're not together as a team, then I can't share that. Then a week later, we're just not able to think about the mistakes we've been making, so we'd make them again. This game is a team game, five against five, so everyone needs to be thinking the same way. Not having the same idea, exactly, but being in tune with each other.

And On to Fnatic

After China, I knew I needed another break. Players come under a lot of mental pressure otherwise. I waited a little while, and then the opportunity to come to Fnatic arose. I want to be a champion, so that's the main reason I came here. And also, I really want to beat South Korean teams with Fnatic at the Worlds. In 2015, Fnatic came up against a South Korean team in the semi-finals of the Worlds, KOO Tigers – they're now called ROX Tigers – but sadly they lost. They were playing really well, though. So I saw how they were performing, and I wanted to be a part of that. I want new experiences, too – like learning English, and trying European culture. I like living in Berlin, it's so nice.

I try to see some of the city when I can. I used to go out with Gamsu, when he was here, every Saturday, and I still try to with other teammates, or players from other teams. I go out to restaurants. It's not boring here at all, and I try hard to maintain a social life. Some players maybe don't have the same kind of work–life balance that I do, but I think it's important.

It was great when Gamsu was here – he joined from Team Dignitas, in the USA, so he had some great experience to bring to the team having played in North

America. Before that, he'd also played for Samsung Galaxy Blue, so I knew him from there. Gamsu's experiences in America meant he could speak English better than me, so he taught me; he also helped me to learn about European culture. He was a big part of my learning process at Fnatic.

The Fnatic fans are amazing. I always get a good feeling from them. After all, if they're not there, then what are we doing this for? We're not pro-gamers unless we're being watched. We're never going to be seen as great at what we do without those fans, and we're not going to have salaries without them, either. And we can always do more for them, to reward their support. Fnatic supporters are always cheering us on. Back when I was in South Korea, when I first started playing, my team had hardly any support at all. So to be here now, and hear the fans in the LCS, it's amazing.

I have headphones on when I'm on stage, and I'm concentrating on the game of course; but when the fans are really going for it, I can hear them, and that motivates me. It fills me with confidence, and makes me want to play with greater flair. It gets rid of any nerves I might have – because even now I do get nervous before the biggest matches, semi-finals and finals in particular.

Now and Next

My mum now, she loves that I have this job. She has great knowledge of video games, and of this game in particular, since I've been playing it at the top level. She actually analyses my performances. She'll speak to me after a game and say, 'Son, this one was wrong, you should have done this.' When I've been on a bad run before, she's said to me: 'Spirit, maybe you should think about retiring.' She's joking around, of course. She's encouraging me to keep going, and to be the best *League of Legends* player. This is what my mum wants for me, and I want it too. I have such great parents.

But I know I can't play for ever. I'm kind of old for *League of Legends* already. My personality has developed so much since I came to Europe from China. And everyone in this team comes from a different place. Now, when I speak to my teammates, I'm always thinking about how they're feeling, and I'm learning too how to care about other people. I'm starting to understand the game at a level above the basic mechanics.

So I think there are a few options open to pro-gamers like me, when we stop playing. I could go into coaching, or streaming. In South Korea, for the LCK, I was asked to be a 'caster only last year. I told them no, at the moment, because I want to continue to be a pro-gamer. But who knows what I will do in the future? Right now, though, I just want to win things with Fnatic.

Spirit's Career in League

Team history

June–September 2013: MVP Blue

September 2013–October 2014: Samsung Galaxy Blue

December 2014–November 2015: Team WE

December 2015–present: Fnatic

Key achievements

May 2014: winner, HOT6iX Championship with Samsung Galaxy Blue

March 2015: runner-up, IEM World Championship with Team WE

December 2015: semi-finalist, IEM Cologne with Fnatic

April 2016: third place, EU LCS Spring Playoffs with Fnatic

11

Top Lane in the Sidelines: Werlyb in His Own Words

It's quite a strange situation to be a substitute here. I'm very hungry to be up there on that stage – before coming to Fnatic, I'd never been the sixth player, watching at the side of the action. But while I want to get up there and show people the level I'm at, I know the team as it stands works really well, and everyone knows each other's game. I want to be here to help the team improve, and to be part of it going forward, but I'm in no rush.

I think Fnatic is much better when it comes to organisation, to discipline, than any other team I've been a part of, but I like that. Before coming here I was at GIANTS!, and at Team Huma, and neither set-up was quite like this.

I'm the sort of player who likes to focus on winning, on taking the game seriously, and if that means three hours more of practice, I will do it. If it means having meetings every day about the drafts, or about our next opponents, I like that, and I want to do it. It's all necessary, when it comes to winning.

The Family That Games Together

I've been playing video games all my life. I've a lot of brothers and sisters, a big family, and we all played them. I would get into *Diablo II*, *World of Warcraft*, and I was really good at the latter at just eight years old. But I didn't start with one specific game, so far as I remember – I just loved games, and played whatever I could get my hands on.

I'm the ninth-born of my siblings, and one of twelve. So I had a lot of older siblings who were encouraging me to get into video games. They would be on them all the time – and they were good, too, which made me want to get as good as them. And when I had the chance, I was playing video games 24/7.

When it comes to *League*, it was one of my older brothers who got me into it, back when it was still in beta, even before the first season. Honestly, I didn't want to play it at first, because I thought it looked boring, but he insisted – 'You *have* to play this game' – and eventually I became hooked on it myself after giving it a chance. I was so bad at first, playing with so few champions, grinding for days to accumulate Influence Points (IP) to buy new ones. Thinking back to when we were all together, playing the same game at home, it was a little like it is in a gaming house today. I didn't follow competitive *League* until quite late, around 2013. Before then, it was about playing with my family.

The first thing about the game that drew me in, once I'd realised it wasn't boring at all, was the fun of seeing each new champion, and playing games both that went well for me, and that I got wrecked in. The emphasis was always on having fun, with friends and family. The more I played, though, the more I wanted to improve, and I began to analyse what I'd done wrong that'd cost me a game – how could I have done that better? – and that competitive edge really began to appeal. It became what I liked about it, and that carried on. I don't know if there was a specific point where I properly began to take *League* seriously, but the more competitive I became, the more I wanted to be.

I had no idea that there were *League* teams just in Spain – I only knew about the Worlds, and a few teams in Europe. But I was playing online alone, going up the rankings, and then a team approached me, called Comando Elite. They weren't very good, but I was so happy to be contacted, because I was used to playing alone. So of course I went for that, and it was such fun to play in a team of five.

Ambitions Realised

When it came to telling my parents I wanted to be a pro-gamer, it didn't feel that hard. I think it affected my father at first. But he came around, and they told me that so long as I was doing well in my studies, and kept social-ising in other ways with friends – actually leaving the house, rather than sitting in front of a screen – then it was okay to really commit to gaming in my free time. So it was never much of a problem for me, convincing my parents this was a career I wanted to pursue, because they could see that I was good, and getting better and better all the time. That could mean something for me, and they were very supportive of my wishes. There were many more pros than cons to going into *League* profes-sionally, and my mum always tells me that if I'm happy, then she's happy.

Coming to Fnatic got my family even more excited than they'd been previously. They knew this was a big team, and for me the move to the Fnatic Academy, after the Spring

Split in 2016, came at a good time because I was having some issues with my previous club, Team Huma, playing in the Challenger Series. But at Fnatic, so far as my parents see it, everything's going to be safe for me, everything's going to be taken care of, so they don't have to worry at all. I'd lived away before, here in Berlin with GIANTS!, so my being away from home didn't worry them, but this time is the best time.

I think everyone understands each other in Fnatic – I get that impression already, having not been here all that long. Everyone shares the same goal: to win. These players don't play for themselves – there's a great feeling of teamwork and harmony. Every week, the feeling is the same: we have to win. And when we don't, there's always discussion about why we didn't. We share our faults with each other in order to improve, and everyone is working hard to be the best they can.

Champion Style

I played as Jax, heavily, early on. I know him inside out. I played him a lot, at a time when nobody was; I got my game so strong. Because I was pretty much the only person using him, a lot of other people assumed he was no good. But I knew differently. I love how he plays – you just go in, and that's my style.

Champion selection is so important. If you're choosing someone whom everyone else is using, when you're learning the game, then everyone you play against is going to know what to expect. They'll have a way of countering what you're likely to do. So it's good to choose something new, or an uncommon champion, whom other people aren't familiar with. They won't know how to play against a surprise, and that can really work.

When it comes to the draft phase, I always liken it to a football match, choosing the team, except you have over a hundred players in your squad. And every one of them has something good about them, and something bad about them. Some are better generally, but who knows, because in a particular game, against a particular team, they might be less effective. The scenarios can vary a lot, so the choices you make in the draft are hugely important. You need to have five players, five champions, who work together, and who can counter what the other team has selected. Perhaps you'll choose a champion purely because they work well with another one, so those two will be part of your team. There's a lot of theory that goes into it – and guesswork as to what the other team will do. Before a game, you might go through a hundred different scenarios as a team – but even then, the opposition can do something you've not planned for, so you have to improvise.

Sometimes, you might not be happy with the champion you've got. It might be one you're not personally comfortable with – but then, it might be one that works better for the team, and for the result. In that situation you have to trust in your teammates, and that while you're not 100 per cent, your team will be.

Role Play

When you're playing competitively, at the top level, you can't play three different roles. You have to specialise, because generally, if you do vary how and where you play, you'll never master any of them. At this level, everyone is so specialised in their role, so if you're splitting your commitment, even between two roles, those players who are just focusing on the one will always have the advantage over you.

I think that's important to remember when you're looking to make steps towards being a professional. You have to focus your game on one role, one lane, and only a few champions. Maybe even just one. When you're always winning with one character, in one role, people will see that and they'll want you to be involved with them, with their team.

I learn a lot from the other people at Fnatic. Like YellOwStaR: he managed to switch roles, from AD carry to support. It's motivating to have these players, players of such a high standard, around me; I've been watching them for a year, learning how they train and how they debate aspects of the game, how they *see* it as well as play it. That's great – these are the best people, so someone like me is always going to learn. But I think they can learn from me, too. I have opinions, and I'll put them forward, and they can stir discussion. I'm able to express my ideas here. I really couldn't ask for anything better, so I have no excuse, really: I have to reach the top level.

People who are good at playing might not understand all of the theory. If you are already good at the game, and then you play a thousand games more, of course you're going to get better – but you might not learn a lot more about the wider game. If you're studying five hundred games and playing another five hundred, then you're actually going to advance that understanding. You'll see how all of these other people play. When it's just you by yourself, constantly practising, all you're actually conditioning is patterns you're familiar with. It's very mechanical. Looking at what other teams are doing will help with your strategic knowledge, and how you communicate with your teammates. I think that's more important than simply working on your own game.

Relieving the Pressure

When I have a day off, if I get the chance, I'll play other video games, or try to go out. But that's only when I'm happy, and the team's happy, and we're performing well. If the team's not doing so well, or I don't feel I'm performing as I should be, I'll use that time for more practice, because I know I need it. And that's not because anyone is telling me to – in fact, people here will tell you when you're practising too much. But if I feel I'm not at my top level, and that I need to improve as soon as possible, then I will play every day. I'll take all the time I need, and in those moments this isn't a job for me: I *want* to get better, and to put that extra effort in. It's not because anyone else is telling me to.

Some people here will only ever play *League*, but I do like to try out other games – just as I have my whole life. Right now I'm really into *Rocket League*, and I'll play online with friends. It's so much fun, and so different from *League of Legends*. I'll also play whatever *Dark Souls* game is out, and the latest *Counter-Strike*. To be honest, I'll play whatever I can, given the chance. I'm a video game fan, not just a professional gamer.

Dark Souls helps me a lot, because it's always killing you, over and over again. That might make you mad, but I actually like that part. I like a game that is so hard, because it makes you take it seriously, and then you get better at it. You don't rest with it, you have to maintain your focus at all times, and that's such good exercise, even on a day off, for playing *League*.

Werlyb's Career in League

Team history

January–December 2013: Comando Elite e-Sports
December 2013–May 2014: Skulls Club
May–August 2014: Dragons
August 2014–December 2015: GIANTS! Gaming
December 2015–April 2016: Team Huma
April 2016–present: Fnatic/Fnatic Academy

Key achievements

November 2013: third place, IeSF World Championship with Spanish national team
December 2014: winner, Liga de Videojuegos Profesional (Spanish league) with GIANTS! Gaming
March 2016: winner, EU Challenger Series Spring Playoffs with Team Huma

12

A New Hope: Kikis in His Own Words

Coming into any new team at the stage of a season like I did, replacing Gamsu in July 2016, is definitely not an easy thing. Fnatic, even with a player missing, was already a very established team, and while changing one player does slightly alter the dynamics, the four of them already knew how to play together. But I think in no time at all we were meshing together well, which is lucky, really – inside a few days of me being there we were all on the same wavelength, when it comes to understanding how we want to play the game. Already I'm able to provide my own feedback in meetings, so that we can tweak what we're doing, and work towards not only getting better, but being the best.

I know Fnatic is one of the biggest teams in the world. I signed a contract with them that takes me into 2017, into next season, and I'm looking to use whatever we achieve in 2016 as a springboard to even more next year. Our results this year will set us up for the next season. I'm delighted to have this opportunity, and will be doing everything in my power to making Fnatic the very best it can be.

Right now, I want to focus on performing as well as I can in 2016, and then hopefully take that into next year's LCS. I also want to further my personal brand, too – but that will come naturally if the team is doing well, with me as a part of it. The team, and performing for them, is always going to be my first priority, but I do like putting time into my social media channels, too.

No Time Like the Present

I knew there'd been some problems with Fnatic's top-laner before I ever received a call. When that call came it was a Friday – and I was in the house, with my stuff, on the Monday. Fnatic's offer was the best I'd had after leaving G2 in June, and it was definitely hard to say no – and to do anything other than come straight into the team because the transfer deadline was on either the Tuesday or the Wednesday of that week. So I got in, signed my contract and jumped straight into the team. The discussions were a little rushed, but then they'd had to be, and I'm happy with the decision.

The second I got to the house, in the early afternoon of the Monday, we had a meeting. I came through the door and literally sat down with the team straight away, in a circle, and jumped right into it. That was a little stressful for about five minutes, because it was a serious talk in a new environment for me. But that lasted for half an hour, and straight afterwards we went into the scrims. So I didn't have much time to acclimatise, I just had to get my gear set up quickly for the scrims.

At G2, I wasn't particularly comfortable with some of the decisions being made by the management. We switched to a six-man team, and the guarantee of a starting spot means a lot to me, so I was feeling kind of undervalued. G2 couldn't guarantee me a starting spot because of promises they'd made to another player there, Expect. I respect them for that, because it's nice that a team cares about all their players – but I had to respect my own feelings. I wish the team and the players all the best, as they're great people, but the time was right for me to leave.

There's a big difference between being at Fnatic and being at G2. For one thing, Fnatic has a far bigger fan base. There's a lot more in the way of expectation on you because of this. I performed well in my first week here, and I had a lot of people writing to me as a result, and that wasn't something I had seen before, not in such numbers. All Fnatic players receive plenty of messages from fans. It makes me happy to see that kind of support. When fans are proud of me, it makes me proud that my hard work is paying off.

Just for Fun

My first experience with games would have been when I was four, and we had an original PlayStation in my old house in Poland. I didn't understand much about it – I'd mostly just watch my older brothers play their games, and they'd sometimes let me have a turn. But I had no idea what I was doing, so I'd simply run around the game at random. My brothers were heavily into video games, so I suppose I got my interest from them.

After that first PlayStation we had a PlayStation 2, and soon after that we got a PC. I just played a bunch of random games – I always enjoyed playing, but not super seriously, and to be honest I wasn't doing it with much commitment.

That changed after primary school, because we moved house – suddenly I was half an hour away from all my friends, and I didn't immediately know too many people locally, so I started to play more games on the PC. Even when I got on to *League*, it wasn't with any intention of taking it seriously. But then after a few months of sticking with it, I felt as though I had something going, that I was genuinely good at it. I wanted to see if I could compete – not for money or anything, just for fun.

I'd played MOBAs before, quite a lot, and I'd put about a hundred games into *DotA* – enough to understand how it worked – and then I came to *League*. So it wasn't too hard to get into, and I was playing with a lot of people who'd never played the game, so I had a bit of a head start against them and immediately felt I was doing well.

I'm not sure what it was, exactly, that hooked me into the game – I guess I just knew it was fun, and playing with my friends at the start was cool. I moved into solo queue, but I had some difficulties to begin with because the PC in my room just didn't want to run the game at all, and I couldn't figure out why for two months. So I had to use my brother's PC, but he'd come home from work at four in the afternoon and kick me off it. I'd try to fit in whatever time I could before he'd come home, and after a few months I realised that I was good.

Attack Is the Best Form of Defence

I'm quite proactive in games. I think I'm probably one of the most proactive top-laners in Europe right now, actually. I'm always looking for opportunities, and wanting to be aggressive in the early stages – when I see an opening, I go for it. I rarely have any doubts about the play in question, but sometimes if my team isn't all on the same page, it doesn't work out so well. I always try to communicate what I'm doing, but I also think outside of the box, and I can adapt how I'm playing in several directions. I've seen my good ideas win many games.

In my very first week with Fnatic, in my first game in the LCS with them, I thought they were playing very passively – and I wanted to change that. So I've been speaking to them a lot, and encouraging them to try new things. Even if these new plays don't work out the first time, or even the second time, you have to keep trying to find new approaches to *League*, to keep ahead of your rivals. We're getting better now at being proactive in games, and I think that will give us an advantage. I want everyone in this team to be seeing every small opportunity and taking advantage of them. For me, attack is definitely the best form of defence.

I'm new to Fnatic, and still fairly new to the LCS compared to the other guys here, but I wouldn't call myself young in terms of playing *League*. I actually consider myself something of a veteran already. Even though I only started playing in the LCS in 2015, I've been around for a long time. I've got so much experience, but it's still a new thing to come into a professional team like this one. And being around the players that Fnatic has means there's always the opportunity to learn more.

That said, I don't think I have too much to learn at this point, but I'm always looking for ways to improve my game, and these guys are great for feeding off, in order to help that happen. Socially, it's good to be around them, too – it's normal for you to pick up personality traits from others. I know what kind of person I want to be, and what I need to work on, so I'm trying to be that – the person who is rock-solid, always reliable, and who cheers other people up. I want to help the other players here however I can.

Positional Expertise

I play top lane right now, but I'm of the opinion that a good, smart player can play in any role, given enough time to practise. Some people are more prone to playing well in one particular role over any others, but I think it's possible for exceptional players to switch between roles over their career.

I personally had enough time to get into top lane, from being a jungler – I played two or three months of solo queue before coming to the LCS, and throughout last season I was always improving in the role. I'm expanding my champion pool, and gaining more knowledge in terms of match-ups against the opposition. The meta is changing all the time, though, so it's always new for everyone. It's not as if you play in one position for three years and you know everything about it – you have to keep up with Riot's patch notes, the changes to the champions, things like that. The way the game is patched can even help a player transition from one role to another, as the champions get reworked and therefore can move from suiting one position to being better in another.

Healthy Body, Healthy Mind

Initially it seemed as though I was incredibly busy when I joined Fnatic, compared to my previous teams. My day was meetings, then scrims, then more meetings, then the gym, and I wouldn't have much time for anything else. I was always playing the game, or thinking about the game. I felt as if all of a sudden I had no time for myself, and that was a challenge to begin with; but I've got used to it, and found more time for myself. That helps me stay healthy, mentally. If you do nothing for yourself for a long period of time, it's going to change you, and when you always need to be communicating with the coaching staff and the players, it's important to keep a strong mind.

I know that, with me, as I've got healthier, I've felt more confident in my body, and that's helped me to feel more confident in everything I do. It affects the way I play *League*, too. Before, I would be more likely to play it safe. So I think being healthy is beneficial to anyone in eSports. Mentally, I guess the gym helps to deal with stress, and it gives me space to think about other things that aren't the game.

Social Enterprise

I'm not the sort of player who can just think about *League* for twenty-four hours, seven days a week. Every Friday I go out with friends and have some fun, maybe some drinks. Other than that I'm at the gym, or at the cinema, and sometimes we'll go out for a meal as a team, or even with other teams. We're all pretty friendly with players of different teams, although you always want to get those bragging rights against an opponent. There's plenty of friendly banter between players on Twitter, inside jokes and things like that. It's always a laugh, and makes each match-up even more fun.

In the house, I've tried to keep up with TV series, but it's hard to make time as when we're here, the focus is almost exclusively on *League*. So the only other thing I do when I'm not out socialising, or playing the game itself, is work on my social media brand. I'm on Facebook, Twitter and Instagram, and I'm always trying to answer the fans. Some people might find that a chore, but I actually like doing it. Even if it's just to say thank you for a kind message, I like to make the effort.

Of course, when it comes to responding to fans, a lot depends on what their motives are. But most of the time, corresponding with fans is a win–win for everyone, because it makes them feel more connected to the team, and makes them happy, and it's good for Fnatic to have its support growing all the time. And of course, you will attract fans who care about you as a player, as the individual, too, and that's great for your own brand, and for your own future in eSports. Look at the top 'casters, as well as the players: they wouldn't be where they are today if they didn't respond to the people who support them. How to behave on social media is a big part of having a career in eSports.

It's hard to be active on social media without having a *reason* to be there, though. If you're a newcomer to *League*, wanting to take things to that next level, then you need to be streaming how good you are – because the best teams will see it. You want to develop a fan base because you're likeable on camera, of course; but if you're no good at the game, you're never going to step from YouTube or Twitch into the professional game.

Kikis' Career in League

Team history

November 2011–May 2014: several teams including Sypher and Denial eSports EU

May–June 2014: Lublin Shore

July–September 2014: SK Gaming Prime

September 2014–July 2015: Unicorns of Love

July 2015–July 2016: G2 Esports

July 2016–present: Fnatic

Key achievements

April 2012: winner, Gamers Assembly 2012 with Sypher

April 2015: runner-up, EU LCS Spring Playoffs with Unicorns of Love

August 2015: third place, EU Challenger Series Summer Playoffs with G2 Esports

April 2016: winner, EU LCS Spring Playoffs with G2 Esports

13

Young Star Ascending: Rekkles in His Own Words

I began playing *League of Legends* in 2010 and started to get my first opportunities in 2012, when I also played my first tournaments with Fnatic. However, at the time I never saw *League of Legends*, or any video games for that matter, as something you could do for a living. I also had other, more important obligations in life, such as school and rehabilitation, as I'd hurt my knee badly when I was thirteen, which stopped me from playing football. I needed an operation for it, and the rehab took a whole year. It was at that time that I started playing *League*. I'd just been into sports before, but I had friends who were into the beta of *League of Legends*, and I thought I'd give it a try.

So I never felt pressured to make it work and pursue things further, playing *League*; rather, I saw it as a rare, but fun, opportunity. It was kind of a win–win situation. It wasn't until I played more seriously that I realised there was a lot more to it than simply taking part in a couple of tournaments here and there while living a 'real life', because playing *was* one. Even though I played back and forth in 2012 and 2013, it wasn't until 2014 that I played my first LCS game and basically 'paused' everything else in life to pursue the opportunity – that's when I felt actual pressure and nerves about the whole thing. So I would say that's when it all started for me.

A Different Kind of Legend

The first-ever video game console I had was a Nintendo 64, around the age of six, back home in Sweden. My favourite games were *The Legend of Zelda: Ocarina of Time* and its follow-up, *Majora's Mask* – to this day I still like to play them, repeatedly. But I wasn't playing them on my own at first.

When I was growing up, my dad had an extreme interest in sports, and would make sure I was properly prepared for my training sessions and, more than that, he effectively coached me. At home, my mum was always interested in video games, and we'd sit and play them together almost on a daily basis when I was young.

So sports, and games, were things I grew up with, albeit one on each side of the family. It wasn't until later on in my life that gaming took a proper hold of me, though, as sports and school were the prime 'subjects', I suppose, in my daily schedule – gaming only ever got a look in when there was time to spare, and then when I injured my knee. I'd almost completely torn my anterior cruciate ligament, and when I did, all the things that'd mattered so much in my life beforehand faded away.

Over the years, *computer* games weren't really my thing, as I spent most of my spare time on console games – first with those Nintendo games, and later on *Call of Duty: Modern Warfare 2* on PlayStation 3, together with my friends once the internet became a 'thing'. However, after my injury, gaming became more and more of a priority as not only did it make me happy, but it also made me forget about everything that had mattered so much to me. As online gaming got more popular, most of my friends moved over to the PC and with *League of Legends* being a free-to-play game, it was just a matter of time.

Like I said before, I grew up in a competitive environment with both sports and games, so regardless of what I was doing, I would always try my hardest at becoming better than the person next to me, and that included *League of Legends*. Therefore I never got to the point where I had to tell myself, 'This is the game for me,' or, 'I'm gonna become the best,' because it happened naturally.

Initially, I was always playing for fun, but when solo queue was going well I realised I was on a different level to my friends. I started playing with professionals, and actually performing against them was when I realised I was just as good as them. I played my first tournament with Fnatic at DreamHack Winter in 2012, and we won it. At that point, even my parents said I should keep doing this. Back then, though, I didn't have the constant pressure of the LCS, and I didn't even understand it. I just thought it was like living in a dorm with people of my own age, with similar interests. At the time I was too young to play in the LCS, as you have to be seventeen, but I'm glad I stayed, and I started playing in the top team here in the fourth season, in 2014.

Attack, Attack

I've played AD carry for Fnatic over the last couple of years – save for some shenanigans in 2015, when I left to play with Elements. I'd established a great relationship at Fnatic with Bora – YellOwStaR – but at Elements I didn't have that same success. It was there that I realised playing with Bora was really good for me, and I wanted to go back to that as soon as possible. I also realised there was a lot more to playing than just being AD carry with any support. I think ever since Bora and I started playing together, we've always done a pretty good job, regardless of who we are playing against.

The name of the role – attack damage carry – basically explains its main purpose: you have to deal as much damage as possible. However, there's a lot more to it and over the years I've come to understand that even though I might be one of the best at just that, *how* you work together with the people around you is what ultimately allows you to reach the highest grounds. That goes for 'outside of the game' interactions as well, with your teammates, as they form you as an individual and the part you play in the coordinated quintet.

The reason why teamwork has become more important over the years is not only because of the scene growing, but because of Riot changing the game in that direction, to encourage cooperation. When I started playing, working together wasn't something you needed to do to win. Even when I went professional, teamwork still wasn't something you thought of – you just went into the games, and had fun, and did your thing. I think it took until season five for me to grasp that it's not just about playing well on an individual level, but how you interact with the people around you, and how you treat your teammates – not only as friends but also as co-workers.

One of the reasons I started maining AD carry to begin with was the release of the champion Vayne in 2011. To this day she's still one of my favourite champions to play due to the 'out of the box' skill set she brings. Even though she hasn't been the most solid AD carry throughout the years, she's always been able to do things others aren't able to accomplish. With that in mind, I wouldn't say she'd be the one to pick up if you're new to the game, as many of the things you want to do with her are related to knowing the game better than your opponent.

Champions like Sivir and Ashe are much more straightforward and a better fit for anyone coming into the game today. When I started playing *League of Legends* back in 2010, Ashe was the one champion I spent the most time on, as she allowed me not only to be effective, but also to learn the game faster as I had to spend less time thinking about the skill set of my champion. I believe that to be the best, though, you'll need to be able to play any champion at any time. But everyone starts somewhere.

Everything But the Game

Whenever I feel down, I try to take an extra step back than I usually do, and do everything that isn't playing *League*. Though when my career started properly, in 2014, I didn't necessarily have any hobbies outside of *League of Legends*, since the game was basically my hobby to begin with. But over the years I've realised the value of actually having something else to take your mind off things, and with me playing a lot of sports at a younger age, going to the gym was a very natural choice.

Another thing I've learned over the past few years of doing this professionally, but perhaps should have appreciated sooner, is that it's always interesting to see how your career develops, and doing what you can to find yourself in a complacent position – both in the game, and in life in general. I don't mean that in a negative way – I mean in terms of feeling comfortable, and not worried about too much. There can be times when it isn't enough, though, and talking to my family is usually what allows me to reset my mind, fully, if the pressure has been on.

Even though we're living different lives, in different countries, talking with my family is something I have to do weekly. They've always been supportive of me, and I've always felt as though I could tell them anything, about any hardship, and they'd try their hardest to put themselves in my position in order to give me the best possible solution. I try to 'pay them back' by going home to Sweden whenever there's an opportunity to do so, even if it's only for a couple of days.

I believe to this day one of the biggest reasons I've never considered going to North America, as many other European professionals have, is due to the importance I place on family. It's already tough as it is, living one hour away from each other by plane – I couldn't imagine how things would be if I were to live on the West Coast of the United States. Perhaps there'll come a day when I change my mind, but for now I'm extremely happy and satisfied with how things are here in Berlin.

National Pride

When it comes to moments in my career to date that stand out, that I'll always treasure, I remember when we played the LCS Summer Finals in Stockholm, in August 2015. I wasn't sure what I could expect, going back home. I never put much emphasis or value on my Swedish fan base, and therefore I expected it to be just like 'any other' finals; but I was blown away by the amount of support I was given.

With the way the games went, and with me having one of my best series, it all ended up being one of my proudest moments so far, not only as Rekkles, but also as Martin Larsson.

I guess at this point I'd have to consider myself famous, and perhaps that became obvious in Sweden. Back in season two, when I started, that was never a goal of mine. Nowadays, usually when you go to events, the fans will come up to you and give you a letter, or a teddy bear, an item that means something to them, and they want to transfer it to you. And it doesn't matter what I'm given, just the fact that I'm given something feels special already. The letters give more context than just a gift, but I've always appreciated everything I've been given.

With us missing out on the finals in spring of 2016, where we finished third, I haven't had a chance to reproduce anything close to that time in Stockholm – but we have a good chance of making it this summer; knowing what I'll miss out on if we don't is heartbreaking. Playing in the LCS is special as it is, but attending those finals is what I'll remember when everything is said and done. Even though 2015 was a great success for us specifically, I believe 2016 has been much more of a learning experience, as it was hard to find any 'issues' when all we did was win up until 2015's Worlds. I personally believe if we'd dropped more games throughout that year, we would've learned more and been a stronger team when it came down to business.

Rekkles' Career in League

Team history

November 2012–April 2013: Fnatic/Fnatic.Beta

May–September 2013: Pride FC

November 2013–November 2014 and May 2015–present: Fnatic

November 2014–January 2015: Alliance

January–May 2015: Elements

Key achievements

November 2012: winner, DreamHack Winter with Fnatic

April 2014: winner, EU LCS Spring Playoffs with Fnatic

August 2015: winner, EU LCS Summer Playoffs with Fnatic

October 2015: semi-finalist, season five World Championship with Fnatic

April 2016: third place, EU LCS Spring Playoffs with Fnatic

14

How to Take Your *League of Legends* Game to the Next Level

*A*dvice from Fnatic players and staff, past and present, on how great casual players can move towards improving their performances, and ultimately knock on the door of the professional scene, or even go beyond it and into a coaching position.

YellOwStaR, Support

I'm still learning, all the time. You always have to visualise how a game could go, meaning that there's a lot of theoretical practice that goes into this profession, into this process. I'd definitely encourage any player to take a good look not just at how they're playing personally, but the wider game, how the matches have been playing out across the map. You think a lot about where you can innovate in a game, where you can be more creative to gain the upper hand. It's all about being able to *see* the games – that's the only thing I can think about.

Losing will always happen. And when it does, it's hard to accept. But usually, after just a few hours, you can move on – what's happened has happened, and you can't change it. The best professionals realise this, and casual players should too. Learn from your mistakes, but don't be too angry at yourself for them, and don't be angry at the game itself. That's the best way to handle it.

You can talk *a lot* in *League*, and that's highly recommended. The more you play, the better you will get at the game, and that's true up to a point. Eventually, though, you have to begin to analyse what you're doing wrong. By looking at your mistakes, and *discussing* them, that's how you improve. You need to understand the mistakes on an individual level, and as a team, and what can be done better in both respects. There is a lot that you can contribute, even outside of the Rift, and you have to be aware of it.

When I started the game, there were not so many champions. Now the game gets updated all the time. It keeps changing. There are new champions all the time. It's important to follow that, and experiment where you can with new champions, but not at the expense of your team's performances.

Your position in a team need not dictate your influence on it: a good captain might normally play support, or be the jungler, as they can move all around the map, but it's all about the personality. When I was at TSM, their mid-laner was very vocal, for example. If someone takes the initiative, it doesn't matter what position they're in. So it's all about the personalities, and leadership happens quite naturally, not necessarily because you're the oldest, or the most experienced in the team.

Rekkles, AD Carry

So for me, the biggest tip I would be able to give someone outside of personal hard work and putting hours of practice in, and studying how certain champions fit each meta, is to put more value than what you tell yourself on the people around you. They're the ones who'll make you stand out; just as how you'll be the one to make them stand out.

As for getting into *League of Legends* as an eSport, as a profession, I'd say with the changes Riot has made throughout the years in terms of 'Challenger Series', it's incomparable to how things were before, where you basically relied on having contacts. These days you can rise up the ladder, prove your worth and eventually qualify to the LCS if you've got what it takes, because every team is watching what's happening in the tier below this one. I guess in some ways, then, you could say I was lucky to get into things when I did. However, as I mentioned before, hard work *always* pays off.

With regards to AD carry in particular, it's a tricky role. It requires a lot of patience, and game knowledge, because you need to know how much damage you can take. But that limit knowledge won't be a factor until you have the mechanical know-how, and that takes a lot of time playing the game and theorising how to do things better. That's actually on you, rather than your teammates – but an AD carry is nothing without their support, so do try to practise with a friend in that role.

Approaching the lane, you need to know how your champion and support match against the other team's selections. You can watch professional streams to see how the lanes are won and lost – a lot of professional streamers will explain what's happening, and why, as they go.

Your power spike is important – different champions have advantages at different levels, so pay attention to that. And when you know you can go for it, do so. That's your time to shine.

In the bottom lane, you're very close to the drake, so pay attention to when that spawns – it can be the difference between winning and losing the game. Getting your last hits in is vital, too, as is coming out on top in team fights, but don't just jump in – it's okay to sit back until that right moment in which you can dash in and pick them all off, and one day score that pentakill. Be patient, and all of this will come with time.

Febiven, Mid-laner

Play with a limited amount of champions. Always watch other people play, and don't get frustrated. Don't talk shit in chat because you're playing bad; that's all on you, and you can control your own emotions. If you're playing with four animals, you'll always have to fight your way through. Watch your replays, and watch other matches. Never get mad.

That said, if people would talk shit at me, I would always flame them back. I know that's bad, but if you have a good resistance to these people, you will just laugh at

197

them instead of getting mad. It means you won't quit the game when someone is talking shit to you – you'll talk shit back.

I think people get put off the game because of what can be said to them, and one way around that is to play with friends. I mean, it's because of my friends that I even started playing *League of Legends*, and playing a game on your own is always less fun than playing with others.

Only play in Summoner's Rift. The other stages are there just for fun, but they won't help you get better, to a professional level. Of course, if you only want to have fun with the game, then you can play wherever you want. It depends what you're looking for.

I'm known as someone who can juke really well, but I don't think I can teach anyone how to do that. You should just try to click as fast as possible, to have that unpredictable movement.

Spirit, Jungler

You have to understand what each lane does to properly work the jungler role. It's knowing the strengths of each lane that will affect your own jungler game. You might play mostly with a strong mid-laner, which gives you the flexibility to be aggressive. You want to tower dive, you can do that, or take a turret, whatever, you can do that – so long as the support is there from your teammates, in the lanes. So understanding what lane is the strongest in any given game is very important.

The second thing is that you shouldn't focus only on one lane, on one way to play – you have to move in 360 degrees. I see some junglers and they're only playing to gank the opposition, or to farm for gold, only this one way. But they need to be thinking about what's the best way to play for their team, as well as for their individual champion. If I'm playing as Lee Sin, I'll have more opportunities to gank, but I should only do it so many times. But if I'm playing as Gragas, I'm going to be more focused on farming, until I'm stronger than the enemy. At that point, you can do whatever you want, within reason, within the team's strengths.

Thirdly, and most importantly, you have to trust your teammates. If you don't, you just cannot play. You will not win games. However well you're playing individually, you will not win a game alone. You need to follow your teammates' calls; and if you see a good opening, you must share it. Communication is so important to the jungler. If the jungler in your team is being quiet, that's not a good jungler.

Kikis, Top-laner

I always tell people three simple things. Play more, of course, that comes first. But second, when you are, *learn* more, by playing with people who are better than you. It's okay to lose games when doing so is making you better.

The third point is to watch replays, and really look at the mistakes you've been making. But basically you can always learn from someone – however good you think you are right now, you're probably nowhere near close to being the best that you can be. And there can only ever be one best player in the world in any position, so almost everyone in the professional game can still learn things. Practise always, and find your limits, and then find out how to go beyond them.

Werlyb, Top-laner

I think if you've no intention to play competitively in *League*, if you're new to it and just want to see how you like it, then I'd play as all of the champions available. You'll find a lot that you like, and you'll probably end up with twenty, maybe thirty that you come back to. I think it's good that there are so many champions to choose from today – but then, I'm not new to the game. Perhaps it's all a bit overwhelming for people just getting started.

Typically, the top lane is the tank role – you're the one who's there to take the damage, instead of your teammates, so you're leading from the front. You want the enemy to hit you as much as possible, not the weaker champions. You can also play AD carries in top lane, and sometimes with mages, but it's really become the place for tanks.

I think the top-laner is a fairly unfashionable role to fill – few newcomers to the game think that's the role for them. But a lot depends on your favourite champions. And you have a lot of options up there, mixing it up between being defensive, and having range. It's definitely the role that allows you to pick the widest variety of champions.

To get better, as a beginner, play with somebody who is not new to the game, so they can show you the ropes. They will be able to show you the basic stuff a lot quicker than the game itself will. They'll help you understand the champions, and what the runes do, otherwise you'll have no idea.

Always try to play with people, not against AI – it's twice as much fun that way. Ideally with friends or family, too, because then you can joke about the ways you might go wrong. Otherwise players you don't know can be quite rude to you, and that can be very annoying. You don't want to feel bullied early on, so always start with people you know.

Understand what kind of role you like, where you want to play, as that way you can buy only the champions who are best suited there. You don't want to waste your Influence Points. If you want to play support, buy support-suitable champions. If you do decide that the top lane is for you, get online and check who's great where. Remember that just because one champion is more expensive than another, it's no guarantee that they're better. That's an easy mistake to make.

Deilor, Fnatic's League of Legends Head Coach, 2015–16

To be a good coach in this game, you don't have to have *League of Legends* expertise, in the mechanical sense that you don't need to know how to be able to execute the moves. You need not understand the game as the players do; rather, you need to get the five players and get the most out of them.

You have to get them understanding systems of play, and each other. You must discipline the kids, and help them to live in an environment with other people, because a lot of these players, they come from backgrounds where they've just been playing at home. They then jump into the professional scene, and they're only very good at the video game – they have no idea how to do anything else in their life. They can click buttons just fine, but they can't do their laundry. So, being a coach in eSports, you have to be a bit of a father figure sometimes, and sometimes a manager. You have to be a strategist, and a psychologist.

When a player disagrees with what we're setting out to achieve, play-wise, we all chip in – the other players get to have a say on what that one player doesn't want to do. I'll ask them: 'Does this make sense?' We all have our opinions, but if the other guys say the opposite to you, then there must be something right about that course of action. So I might have an opinion about something in the game, and while I'm pretty stubborn, everyone here is able to offer an opinion. If all the players say that I'm wrong, I will accept that – even if I think I'm right.

And I'm wrong on a daily basis, because I'm taking more shots than anyone. My goal in the team was to get it to perform, and to get it to perform it needs to evolve; for it to evolve, we need to *try stuff*. And that means you will be wrong, constantly. But the thing is, I don't really mind being wrong. I'm okay being wrong. Most people aren't like that. If I say something, and then one of the players answers me, and through that we get new information, then my failure is actually a win. The team has learned something, and with this new information, we add it to the pool of what we know already, and then we've reached a new strength.

Patrik Sättermon, Fnatic's Chief Gaming Officer

One of the aspects of this book is to be educational, so a message to younger players is definitely to take care of your brand, and your public level of awareness, be that running a YouTube channel or live-streaming. You need to be out there and engaging with people – that can definitely help. Obviously the focus has to be on being a great player, but being active on social media never hurts. And going out, and meeting people. Be sociable with this game – it's not about staying in and committing every hour to the Rift.

The beautiful thing about eSports is that everything is trackable online, so we can find these people, the best out there in levels beneath the LCS. You hear those stories in traditional sports, or music, about a team finding a guy on a beach and signing them up, or a label hearing a new artist on YouTube and doing the same – and that happens on a way more frequent basis in eSports. All of that data is out there, online; it's just a question of interpreting it and tracking the rising talents.

At Fnatic, we're always looking for people who are, pardon the pun, fanatical about what they do. We want players who are committed to reaching the very highest level, not just in eSports but in terms of their own lives. Are they willing to put a lot of time into this? They'd better be, because we demand that of our players. That's a side to being part of Fnatic, the commitment to it – but we encourage passion, too, and a sense of being part of a team, competing in something together. And that really cuts to the heart of what eSports is.

We don't really have any core values, as such, as we're a global team, maybe more than any other organisation out there. And with that comes an openness to how we coach, depending on the territory we're in, and the people we're dealing with. We work with both introverts and extroverts, people who are yin and yang – you can find them all at Fnatic. But the thing that connects them is that great passion, and the mind for competition, and sportsmanship.

Every one of our players wants to be the best, but we also like them to exhibit modesty. If you come in and win a tournament straight away, you might think it's the greatest thing that's ever happened to you. But then your career might fall off very soon, and if you've been arrogant about it, you might not be the most liked guy around. That can damage your future in the game.

We want players to look at where Fnatic is today, and to learn from the past. We're not ruling out bringing in one-on-one titles at the company, but historically it's team games that have provided us with more stability and more recognition, so if anyone is looking to attract our attention, it's in those games like *League, CS:GO, DotA 2, Heroes of the Storm* and now *Overwatch*. We don't have to rely on one person to create Fnatic's legacies – this is like a Premier League team, and we want it to go on for a long time. But all of these different games, one-on-one titles included, contribute to the great world that is eSports.

15

The Future of Fnatic, its Fan Relationships and *League of Legends*

*L*eague of Legends has received what feels like countless patches since its launch, and as its players both at the top level of the game and simply playing for fun with their friends state with equal authority, this is categorically not the same game it started as.

'To put the significance of these patches in context, consider football,' says Deilor. 'You know how the game is played right now, what shape the goals are. But now, imagine that the rectangular goals become triangular. And then you take the pitch, which looks the same as it did before in terms of the markings, but now you make it so that the edges of it curve downwards, so the ball will always run away from the centre. And the football itself has its shape changed just a little bit, so that it bounces weirdly. That's what it's like when *League of Legends* gets patched. It's the same game, *but it's not*, as there will be all of these changes that alter what you knew. And this happens all the time, which sounds crazy in the context of traditional sport, but for *League of Legends* it's normal.

'I honestly don't think that *League of Legends* will be here in twenty years,' continues Fnatic's former head coach. 'The whole eSports scene will continue to expand but the games won't remain the same. You look at a game like *StarCraft II*, which was huge not so long ago, but is now fairly small. *Counter-Strike* and *DotA* are still popular, but in their newer versions. I guess a *League of Legends 2* is the next step to take, to keep the game popular. But I don't know if Riot would do that, given that this game is being patched all the time anyway. If the game *is* still around in twenty years, that would be awesome, but I think it's part and parcel of the evolution of technology – which gaming is always such a servant to – that it won't be.'

Staying Competitive

Fnatic doesn't remain in a state of stasis when it comes to the games it supports – that much was clear when it brought in a *League of Legends* team in the first place. It's still evolving today, confirming the acquisition of an *Overwatch* team in July 2016, comprised of former Nubris players, a mix of highly rated Americans and Swedes.

'The way we look at our team acquisitions is to respect that we need a diverse roster, to reflect how new games come into relevance,' says Patrik Sättermon. 'The way that technology progresses all of the time, the younger generation always expects new forms of entertainment. There are so many games to keep an eye on. You don't need to be a rocket scientist to recognise that the eSports landscape can change very quickly, whereas a more traditional sport like football might not change much over a hundred years.

'We have a fairly high threshold for getting into a new game, though. It needs to be a *good* game, obviously, and also have a strong existing player base. We look at the approach of the game developer in question – is what they're doing new, and exciting? If we can see a future in the game, and find players of it that share our values, then we can move forward. There's no perfect equation for how we go into any new game, as there are many different perspectives to consider, on a case-by-case basis. A lot of it comes down to a gut feeling, and also the legacy that the developer might already have established.

'With *Overwatch*, you have the history of its developer, Blizzard, that can't be ignored, and its unique fusing of gameplay, with the MOBA styling and the first-person shooter qualities. It's done in a fascinating way, and in a extremely *successful* way when you look at just how big the game is already. So *Overwatch* is a very natural progression for us.

'When it comes to *League of Legends*, I think it's probably already hit its peak, in terms of popularity, but it has many years of success ahead of it, too. Riot is doing a great job when it comes to operating the game as an eSports title, and they probably have the best ecosystem when it comes to how the game's professional side is structured, with the different leagues and a well-run transfer market. That's something that a lot of other organisations lack.

'So while I think that *League*'s probably already had its moment where the most people possible are excited for it, it's certainly not about to disappear tomorrow. Over time, though, it's natural that there will be a decline – which will be countered by other projects coming online, and investment in other areas of eSports. It's going to be interesting to see how Riot takes the huge success of *League* into what they do next, because I think what they've done, for MOBAs, is better than anyone else.'

The Fan Factor

'We have some really passionate supporters,' says Sättermon. 'I've been in the States, in Asia, all over the world, and the support that Fnatic receives is always phenomenal. Fans can get crazy, really hyped.'

One such fan is Douglas Rutan, of Westland, Michigan. He's been following Fnatic's *League of Legends* team since the third season. 'Back then, my home region of North America wasn't very strong in a global sense, so instead of watching a weak league, I started to watch the EU teams,' he says. 'The personalities in the Fnatic team at the time – sOAZ, xPeke, Cyanide – they were really easy to like, and their team was so strong that supporting them was a kind of bandwagon move for me. But it was the team's support, YellOwStaR, who's been an inspiration to me – he improved himself personally, losing a lot of weight, and achieved world praise in a role that he wasn't native to.

'Supporting Fnatic is a big deal for me, because I have a lot of respect for the organisations that were in there, involved in eSports, before it became an easy investment opportunity. The original teams from the NA and EU LCS splits risked so much, and without their efforts the eSports industry, and *League of Legends*, would be a fraction of the size it is today. Most people don't take eSports seriously, so

211

supporting a team that plays video games does seem odd to them – but I love wearing my Fnatic gear around.

'I think Fnatic is good to its fans, too. They opened an NA store, which gives fans over here free shipping. Their Twitter account is always active, letting you stay up to date on their management and coaching activity, and when they're playing next, so you don't miss a game. I definitely believe that Fnatic treats its fans as priority number one, which could be why the team has lasted so long.'

Sättermon says: 'I think that the successes we've had, and the superstars we've had on our teams, have helped us to generate a strong fan base. But I also want to attribute that to our early moves into live-streaming, and our active social media attitude. Early on, other organisations weren't so active as us, and that means that we have tens of millions of fans across all of our social media channels, and a few million people per month tuning in to our live streams. It's something that's hard to get right, because there's a never-ending stream of comments coming in to us, but then we are a 24/7 organisation, with players spread across different time zones. We have to be mindful of that, and respect how people are interested in us and want to reach out, and we'll always do our best to respond to the community however we can. We have a genuine respect for our fan base.'

'YellOwStaR and Rekkles are definitely superstars,' says Rutan. 'I have friends who claim that Rekkles being at the team is the reason they stick with Fnatic. Personally, I like Febiven's style of play more. I think he's following in the footsteps of YellOwStaR and Rekkles, and is only a few years behind them. He's possibly even the most talented player on the team, because he hasn't peaked yet, while the other two probably have. However, I wouldn't like to pick a favourite player in the team – they're all great, and I'm hoping to meet them when they next come to my part of the world.'

Battle of the Sexes

Earlier in the book, you perhaps noticed Patrik Sättermon use 'him or her' in regard to player acquisition, and while there is no female player in Fnatic's premier teams at the time of writing, this is something the organisation, like many in eSports, is not ruling out for the future.

'There's certainly no ruling on not having mixed-sex teams,' says Finlay Stewart. 'We *can* have a girl player. The problem so far is that we've not seen any who are at the level we're looking for. That's not a sexist thing – this is all about having the talent. If a girl player were as good as, or better than, our players, we would instantly take her.

'I know that this is a sensitive topic, but there's nothing stopping any team in the LCS from recruiting female players. We have seen it before in *League*, in the US, where a girl has been on a team that's done really well. I do worry, though, that if someone broke through in the European LCS, it might be seen as a novelty, and treated negatively – you have to remember that the demographic for this game is something like 80 per cent teenage males, and that means it's going to take a long time before we see a lot of female players emerging.

'Girl players have a very big opportunity to make a living without going pro, though, through streaming and YouTube, and the amount of negative attention they'd, sadly, inevitably receive in going pro is a big barrier. You would have to be so confident to come into this male-dominated scene, and not give a shit about what people say about you, because you would get a lot of garbage. The opinions that are always the loudest are those of the trolls – those who are accepting, or simply don't care, aren't the ones posting comments.

'It's always great to see more girls in the audiences for the LCS, though. I hope the game has a drama to it that can appeal to everyone, whether or not they play themselves. For example, my mum likes football, but she's never played the game in her life.'

The female player to whom Stewart refers is Maria Creveling, aka 'Remi', who in August 2015 was part of the Renegades team that won promotion into the NA LCS from the Stateside Challenger Series, making her the first female player in the LCS, in either territory. She is still with the team, in the support role (her champion of choice is Thresh, leading to fans calling her the Thresh Goddess), but upon rising to the American top division she was unsure of whether or not to take her professional career further – a feeling perhaps stirred because of the fear of receiving sexist discrimination from a small section of the *League* audience.

She posted on the Renegades subreddit, soon after the team's promotion:

> The competition doesn't mean much to me. I don't care to be the best in the world . . . When I set out . . . I wanted to be the first girl in LCS. That was what motivated me. That dream I had I accomplished and yet it is being challenged in such a heartless way . . . Everyone that tries to take away from what I accomplished, well, I will always spite them.

Remi was responding here to the numerous forum and social media posts that she wasn't born a girl, and therefore cannot claim to be the first female in the LCS. She continued in her subreddit post: 'I just want it to be known that I accomplished my goal for real, and I accomplished it for me, my teammates, and girls in eSports. That's it. No one else. Don't . . . put me on some LGBT agenda or some bullshit and bring that up.'

Countless messages of support swayed Remi's perspective on competing in the LCS, though, and the team finished eighth in the 2016 Spring Split. And her achievement certainly should be an inspiring one. While *League* has seen an all-female team attempt to reach the top level before, with America's Team Siren – comprised of outstanding solo queue players on the NA servers, forming in May 2013 only to disband weeks later due to conflict between the starting five – it's a discipline, much like any eSport, that should not discriminate based on gender.

There's no reason whatsoever that tournament-winning teams can't be made up of girls and guys. If you're good enough, you're good enough, and competitive gaming, across the entire industry, needs to stay open to women making it beside the men. There are countless articles online investigating why women are yet to truly break into eSports, and they consistently arrive at the same verdict: sexism. Speaking to PCGamesN in 2015, Selfless Gaming's *CS:GO* player Heather 'sapphiRe' Mumm commented: 'If

I stumble . . . it's: "Go back to the kitchen. You shouldn't be playing." If we got sponsorship and I got a mouse pad? "You don't deserve that mouse pad. A better team deserves that mouse pad." Every little thing.'

The Press Perspective

Wherever eSports goes next, the growing media circus around it is certain to follow. Yahoo eSports' Michael Martin has been following competitive gaming for several years, for additional outlets such as IGN, *PC Gamer* and GamesRadar+, which makes him well positioned to speculate on what the industry's Next Big Thing might be. Fortunately for Fnatic's immediate future, he agrees with Sättermon that *Overwatch* is going to become a serious player on the eSports scene.

'If we're talking eSports overall, its really hard to deny that games like *League of Legends*, *DotA 2* and *CS:GO* aren't the biggest games around. The scope and money involved in those games is significantly bigger than anything happening in the competitive fighting game community, or tournaments featuring traditional sports sims.

'In terms of what's next, though, *Overwatch* might be the next game primed to "make it big" in eSports. In my opinion, *Heroes of the Storm* [*HotS*] doesn't seem to have the legs to compete with games like *LoL* and *DotA 2*, but Blizzard – the company that makes both *Overwatch* and *HotS* – is putting a lot of resources to make *Overwatch* a phenomenon, both in and out of eSports. Its setting and lore seems tailor-made for movies, cartoons and merchandising. As an eSport, however, Blizzard has to be careful with its newer game, which people are calling a "hero shooter". Maintaining competitive balance with so many characters, while adding new ones as it progresses, is a tall task. But if there's any game on the horizon that can wedge itself into the upper echelon of eSports games, *Overwatch* is probably it.'

'I think what's really exciting,' says Julia Hardy, BBC presenter and journalist, 'is just the whole idea of competitive play, and seeing it as an interesting way to spend your time. And there are more and more games right now producing some good multiplayer experiences – *Overwatch*, for example, has been monumental. But there's a lot of scope to encompass games aimed at younger players in eSports – London's Gfinity venue, for example, has run *Splatoon* competitions. You're starting to see a greater breadth in terms of the type of game that could be played competitively, games that can be legitimately called eSports.

'I'm on this complete mission to do an eSports event that's for the whole family. So you'll have a *Mario Kart* cup for the dads because, come on, *every* dad thinks they're good at *Mario Kart*. And everyone likes to compete, I think, so that would be nice. And I think that this whole thing can only grow. And once you have broadcasters like Sky Sports being involved, and the BBC doing more, then you have that top-tier respected programming, and that'll be exciting. It feels like there's a wealth of opportunity and potential out there, and people are coming into eSports all the time.

'In every meeting I have, eSports is the buzzword. I'll go into production companies and they're all, "We *must* do something with eSports." So this snowball effect is happening. How mainstream channels and traditional production companies are going to pull it all together, I don't know. But it's about breaking through this idea that there's just one kind of gamer, and I think once broadcasters, and the media in general, get past that, we'll see tailored programming for all kinds of gamers, because the gaming audience is just as diverse as music fans, and film fans. Once they get to that and make programming that's more selective, I think everything is going to become more interesting, and more diverse. It's a lovely position to be in.'

'Plenty of games are now designed with eSports in mind,' says Martin. 'But it isn't the developers who ultimately decide if a game is eSports. It's the community. *Rocket League* has had incredible success in eSports, and I doubt anyone expected that, but I'm not sure it will go beyond being a niche eSport, and reach the level of *League of Legends*, or *CS:GO*. Publishers, developers and sponsors have to contribute to a game's success in eSports. Games like *Duelyst* – a fantastic card-/grid-based strategy game, similar to *Hearthstone* – or *The Culling* – a sixteen-player first-person arena combat game (it's a bit like *The Hunger Games*, the video game, where the last man standing takes all) – would make great eSports titles. But if these never become "true" eSports, its because the *community* didn't accept them as eSports, not because they're bad eSports games.'

Prolonging Careers, and Seeding New Ones

The average age of a pro-gamer is around twenty-two. Many begin their careers at seventeen or eighteen – Rekkles is an exception, brought into Fnatic at a younger age and supported until he was old enough to compete in the LCS – and leave the top divisions in their mid-twenties. 'A young man's game' were Febiven's words in Chapter 9. Outside of the elite, the players earning a living from gaming, the average age is higher – thirty-three years old in Australia, for example, due to the long history of multiplayer titles like the *Call of Duty* and *Counter-Strike* series.

'I think any pro-gamer reaching close to the age of thirty can admit that they can't compete with the reflexes or speed of gamers that are much younger,' says former Fnatic player Tim 'WetDreaM' Buysse, now thirty-one and retired from competitive gaming. 'But the advantage older players have is experience and knowledge; they will probably make better decisions.

'I also think there is another problem when you get older than the age of twenty-five, and that is *real life*. If you never have dreams or expectations of getting a normal life you can keep gaming for as long as you want, but for me at least there was always more to life. I want to have kids, a house, see my family as much as I can, and it's hard to get that as a pro-gamer. I enjoyed my time gaming, for sure, and I don't regret it; but I wouldn't go back to it because I am a much happier person with the life I have now.'

For so-called senior players in the LCS, where they go after their playing career is over is becoming a serious matter of consideration. At twenty-four, YellOwStaR is weighing up what's ahead for him, aware that he can't maintain his present level of play for ever – and one thing he really aspires towards is showing that eSports, and gaming in general, isn't an unhealthy pastime.

'When some people think of video games, or the players of video games, they might still think of the guy in their dark room, door closed. They have no social life. And this was the image we had decades ago. Now, I want to be a role model for eSports, that parents who have no idea what it's about can look to if their children want to get into it. Parents ask me all the time now about eSports, but ten years ago they'd have just laughed about it. Now they're more open, asking me what I'm doing, and you explain all the aspects. This is a lot more than just playing video games! There's the interviews, the media, everything else.

'If I look back at how I was before starting eSports, compared to where I am now, I would say that I have come a long way, and have grown a lot. And I want to write my own book, that's a point of reference for other people, to know what it's like to do this. I want parents to have something to look at, to understand when their own son or daughter is in the same situation. It's all becoming more and more professional.

'Inevitably, sometimes other things get in the way of your gaming career, and take priority; and also there is so much pressure that some players do just burn out. You have to be really reactive in many situations. You have to be on point in regard to the general mechanics, but that takes a lot of time every day, to stay sharp. I don't see myself playing ten, fifteen hours a day in three years' time.

'Before I started, my parents always wanted me to have a stable future, and I would say today that I've been lucky. I've never had to work a "proper" job, and I've never worn a suit to work. Now people are coming into eSports younger and younger, without even graduating from school, and lots of parents, and the media, are wondering what these people are going to do after eSports, because there is no job security. Say you don't perform, and you've been playing for three months – what are you going to do then? Perhaps you've wasted a whole year. Maybe it's an experience that's worth it – but what next?

'I've been thinking about whether or not I want to stay in eSports, because for me, when I was younger, my vocation was being a doctor. But I don't see myself going back to school now to study for ten years. That is a long process. So I'm deciding whether or not to stay in eSports, and if I do, in what capacity. I'm unsure about what I really want to do, but I think I want to stay in eSports.'

The Fnatic Academy is a way in which the team can bring new *League* hopefuls into their system, and monitor their progression with a view to introducing them into the main LCS team. It's been an on-and-off arrangement, but as of the spring of 2016, the Academy is running again, based around the team's support Klaj, who turned out in the LCS in early 2016, prior to YellOwStaR's return.

'The Academy is something we toy around with from time to time,' says Sättermon. 'In *League of Legends*, it's allowed us to provide younger players with a tournament structure, and organisation, that is really valuable to their development. We felt that replicating a lot of the things we do with our top team with the Academy team would really make sense, and help improve that younger talent under-neath the Fnatic umbrella. We've a few of the Academy players living with the pro-players in Berlin, like Werlyb and Klaj. And that obviously increases that connection between the players, and helps the substitutes step in if they need to for a week.

'Looking at this from a business approach, the Academy allows us to keep attracting fresh talent, and to remain this successful. As eSports grows, we'll see a lot of conven-tional sports teams getting involved, which increases the competition for the best talent out there. So the Academy is acknowledging that future and tackling it face-on, using the facilities we have to bring our own talent through, from very early stages in their careers. That will give us some natural options when it comes to necessary replace-ments, and also an advantage in the transfer market when it comes to helping players find other teams. We're not comfortable in bidding wars, but we know that in the years to come it'll be hard to not have to go through that, so we need to intensify our efforts when it comes to protecting our talent.

'Fnatic has been able to foster talent right through the eSports era. This industry isn't one where you can just pop into the local library and learn all about it – it's all about evolving as you do it, through trial and error. We've not always had winning teams in every game, but if you look at all the eSports verticals, together, and compare them to other organisations, nobody even comes close to what Fnatic has achieved. Talent breeds talent, and success fosters more success. We have a great hall of fame, we're a team that players want to come to, we have the most amazing fans, and I know we're the most successful team out there, across the board.'

A Beginner's Guide to *League of Legends* Terminology

*L*eague of Legends has a language of its own within eSports, which can be incredibly confusing for newcomers. What follows is a basic glossary covering some of the terms appearing in this book, and is by no means comprehensive. A recommended destination for anyone wanting to learn more is the *League of Legends* Wiki, at leagueoflegends.wikia.com, which features a regularly updated guide to the words used by players, streamers and 'casters alike.

Abilities

Every champion has their abilities, skills unique to them, which cost mana to perform. Over the course of a game, every champion will unlock, or learn, four abilities. The fourth to activate is called the 'ultimate' ability, their defining move and usually their strongest.

AD *carry*

The AD carry position in a *League of Legends* team is a champion who is selected for maximum enemy damage. These champions deal out consistently powerful attacks, but they might not have the best defence. For this reason, the AD carry role is usually run in tandem with the support role – the support player ensuring that the AD carry is kept alive and suitably buffed.

Attack damage (AD)

The AD figure is the amount of health a champion takes off their enemy with each blow. There is a base figure, and a bonus one – the latter is affected by the use of runes, of buffed abilities.

Auto attack (AA)

A basic attack, performed by a champion to deal damage to an enemy, activated by a right click in close proximity to the opposing avatar. They generally cannot be dodged.

Bans

In the draft phase of each pro-level game, when players select their champions, each team can ban the other from using up to three champions, leading to six bans in total for any single game. This affects team strategies, sometimes leading to on-the-fly plays, and highlights why the pros have to be proficient across a variety of champions.

Baron Nashor

Baron Nashor is the most powerful natural monster in Summoner's Rift, first spawning at twenty minutes into each game. Destroying the Baron rewards the whole team that conquers it with a powerful buff, Hand of Baron, increasing attack damage and increasing ability power.

Bottom lane

The bottom lane is usually home to the AD carry and support champions.

Brush

If a player is in the brush of a map, an overgrown area, they are in stealth and invisible to the opposing team until they leave it or the enemy uses a sight-granting ability.

Buffing

When a player's champion is buffed, they have received a beneficial status effect, raising health, attack damage or the power of their special abilities. Most in-game buffs are temporary. When a champion loses power, this is debuffing.

Challenger Series

The Challenger Series is the tier of competitive play directly beneath the LCS. It is at the top of a ladder that begins at an unranked level and moves through Bronze, Silver, Gold, Platinum, Diamond and Master levels, before reaching Challenger. Where a player competes is dependent on their League Score (LP).

Champion

Champions are *League*'s player-controlled characters. They come in a cornucopia of classes, shapes, sizes and fantasy races.

Cheese

A cheese is a high-risk play that could swing a game in your team's favour or totally lose it. It can also mean when a team carries out an unorthodox play, one that might not be considered in the spirit of the game – hence, it 'cheeses' the opposition off.

Creeps

The creeps are the AI-controlled minions in the game. They can be assigned to any lane, and will attack the opponent until they are destroyed.

Crowd control effects (CC)

These are abilities that affect an opponent's own abilities, either individually or in a group. They are a means of debuffing the enemy. CCs come in many different varieties.

Draft

The draft is the pre-game selection of champions, factoring in team strategies and responding to bans.

Dragons/drakes

The dragon – which appears as four different elemental drakes across the course of a game – is the second-most-powerful neutral monster on Summoner's Rift. During the first thirty-five minutes of a game, one of four of these elemental monsters will spawn every six minutes – Cloud Drake, Infernal Drake, Mountain Drake and Ocean Drake. Defeating each one rewards the team with unique 'dragon slayer' buffs.

At thirty-five minutes, the Elder Dragon spawns – defeating this enhances all previously attained dragon perks.

Duo queue

If you're playing duo queue, you're competing in ranked games with a friend, but in games where others are entering solo.

Farming

Farming is the act of destroying multiple minions/creeps in-game to gather gold. Many players farm early in order to buy the best items for use later in the game.

Field of Justice

The in-game terminology for the maps the games are played out on.

First blood

The first champion to slay another champion achieves first blood. First blood rewards the team in question with bonus gold, compared to regular kills.

Gank

A gank is an overwhelming surprise attack on the enemy that can wipe them out. It usually covers when a champion from one lane, or the jungle, moves elsewhere to join a team fight, to increase that team's chances of winning.

GG

Acronym for 'good game', usually exchanged between online players at the end of a game. Not to be confused for 'git gud', on account of this not being *Dark Souls*.

Gold

Gold is the in-game currency of *League*. Teams will collect as much as they can and take it to their shop, based at their home Nexus. Here, they can exchange gold for bonus stats and abilities. This is one of the main ways a champion levels up, and increases in strength, during a game.

Health

Health is the green bar on the HUD (head-up display). If yours falls to zero, your champion falls, and will respawn after a set amount of time, depending on various circumstances, ranging from ten to over fifty seconds.

Howling Abyss

A single-lane *League of Legends* map with no jungle area.

Influence Points

Influence Points are awarded to each player after a game, the amount depending on how well they have performed. They are not bought with real money. They can be exchanged for new champions and runes.

Items

Teams exchange gold for items at shops. These improve each champion's stats on the map, and can cover attack or defence perks, increased mobility, or reduced cooldown between abilities.

Juke

To juke is to fake an opposition player out, trick them into thinking you're about to do something but then you don't, or to simply dodge their abilities. It can also basic-ally mean escaping from the enemy.

Jungle

The jungle is home not only to the jungler, but also *League*'s nastiest neutral monsters, which don't fight for either team and can be farmed for gold and experience. The jungle is only found in Summoner's Rift and Twisted Treeline.

Jungler

The jungler is the champion/player focusing on harvesting the gold from neutral monsters.

Lanes

Summoner's Rift is split into three lanes – top, middle and bottom. It is through these that creeps/minions progress towards the enemy's base. Other maps, those not used professionally, have different layouts of lanes.

Lane swapping

When the champion in the top lane switches with those in the bottom lane. Hard to pull off successfully but if timed right can pitch a powerful and well-supported AD carry into a head-to-head with an opposition top-laner yet to level up sufficiently, opening a path to the enemy Nexus.

Last hitting

Getting the killing blow in on a creep is essential to your team's gold count. This means not auto-attacking, but waiting for the enemy minion's health to be as good as gone and then whacking them into pieces.

LCS

The LCS is the *League of Legends* Championship Series. It covers leagues and tournaments in Europe and North America, with ten teams on each continent. These teams play each other once, across nine weeks, and the top six teams in each league then go into knockout-style playoffs. The top three teams in each league qualify for the annual *League of Legends* World Championship.

League of Legends World Championship

This is the big one, representing the culmination of seasons across the world. Sixteen teams qualify in total (in 2015, this was three each from Europe, North America, China and South Korea, two from elsewhere in Asia, and two international wildcards), going into four groups. The top two teams from each group progress into the quarter-finals. Eight teams become four for the semi-finals, before a grand final determines the world champion for the year in question.

League Points

The number of League Points you have, as a player in solo or duo queue, or as part of a team, determines where you stand in the ladder beneath the LCS (and equal-level competition). You win points for playing in ranked matches, which are always contested on Summoner's Rift.

Mana

Mana is the resource used to cast spells and use abilities. It is represented by the blue bar on the game's HUD (head-up display).

Mid-laner

The mid-laner is the champion/player focusing attacks and defence on the middle lane.

Minions

See 'Creeps'.

Nerf

The 'nerfing' of a champion, or any other aspect of *League*, is when a patch deliberately weakens them, to achieve a better overall balance to play.

Neutral monster

In *League*, it's not just the opposition team that poses a risk to your health – the maps are also full of monsters.

Get too close to them and they will attack. Defeat them for gold. Monsters spawn in the jungle.

Nexus

The Nexus is the crystal-like structure at the heart of each team's base. Destroy the enemy's Nexus, and you win the game. Minions are spawned from the Nexus, and champions revived there. They are protected by turrets.

Patches

These are regular updates to *League*, made by Riot, to better balance the game. The details of each update are always posted to the official *League of Legends* website: leagueoflegends.com

PC bang

A LAN (local area network) gaming centre, typically found in South Korea, where patrons pay a small fee for playing video games either locally with friends or online.

Rift Herald

The Rift Herald is another powerful neutral monster in Summoner's Rift. It occupies the same position on the map as Baron Nashor, who only spawns after twenty minutes, after which time the Rift Herald does not return.

Riot Points

Riot Points are an in-game currency acquired with real money. They can be exchanged for new champions and skins, or modifiers to increase the rate of collecting Influence Points.

Runes

Runes are earned enhancements to a champion that any player can collect and use prior to a game. They are purchased from the Riot Store using Influence Points. There are four kinds of rune: mark (offensive), glyph (magical), seal (defensive) and quintessence (utility).

Scrim

When pro teams are scrimming, they are competing in prearranged five-versus-five matches, but outside of competitive play (in the LCS, for example). Usually, scrimming happens in preparation for competitive play.

Shoutcaster

A shoutcaster is someone who commentates live on competitive eSports. As per the term, they can get fairly lively.

Sight

You have sight when you can see, or have vision of, an area of the map. When you do not, and it remains obscured, it is said to be covered in 'the fog of war'. Sight can be an ability used by champions, particularly those in the support role, to get a wider read on the state of the game.

Skill shot

A skill shot is an offensive champion ability, usually a projectile, which can be aimed and fired at an enemy, or several. They travel in straight lines.

Solo queue

This is you when you're waiting to join a game all on your lonesome. This is how a lot of professionals started, and learned the ropes of *League*.

Summoner

The summoner in a game of *League* is you, the player, who controls a champion.

Summoner's Code

The rules and regulations by which *League* players are expected to abide, or else face fines and bans from Riot.

Its nine key points are: support your team; drive constructive feedback; facilitate civil discussion; enjoy yourself, but not at another player's expense; build relationships; show humility in victory and grace in defeat; be resolute and not indignant; leave no newbie behind; and lead by example.

Summoner's Cup

The in-no-way ostentatious trophy awarded to the world champions every year.

Summoner's Rift

The main map used in *League of Legends*, and in all top-tier competitive play, comprising three lanes and a wide jungle area.

Support

The support player in a game of five against five is there to literally look after their teammates, especially the AD carry, who they will usually share the bottom lane with. This involves healing and buffing, warding (seeing more of the map, to gain an advantage) and helping the carry get extra kills.

Swag

Promotional materials – toys, gadgets, literature, inflatables, whistles, glow sticks, silly hats – given out to fans at eSports events. It can be handed to attendees on the way in, or thrown into the crowd between games.

Tanks

Tank champions are designed to soak up enemy attacks, provoke battles and prevent their weaker teammates from taking too many hits.

Team fight

This is when the minions aren't much of a factor any more and the player-controlled champions are simply beating the hell out of each other.

Tilt

If a player says they are 'on tilt', it means they are experiencing a drop in form and making a lot of mistakes. It's basically bad luck, albeit influenced somewhat by a player's inability to control their emotions during a game.

Top-laner

The top-laner is the champion/player focusing on the top lane in Summoner's Rift. This has become a place where tank characters face off.

Turrets

Also known as towers, these static defensive posts block the enemy's progress to the Nexus. They can only target one champion at a time, meaning that teamwork is required to take them down. Minions cannot progress towards an enemy Nexus until the turret in their lane is destroyed. There are eleven turrets per team on Summoner's Rift, and fewer on the other maps.

Twisted Treeline

A two-lane *League of Legends* map with a jungle area. The jungle here is home to Vilemaw (the map's take on Baron Nashor), an undead spider with a penchant for bad dancing (look it up on YouTube).